Strategic Managerial Accounting—A Primer for the IT Professional

Strategic Managerial Accounting—A Primer for the IT Professional

Gopal Saxena, PhD

BEP BUSINESS EXPERT PRESS

Strategic Managerial Accounting—A Primer for the IT Professional

Copyright © Business Expert Press, LLC, 2017.

First published in 2017 by
Business Expert Press, LLC
222 East 46th Street, New York, NY 10017
www.businessexpertpress.com

ISBN-13: 978-1-63157-583-9 (paperback)
ISBN-13: 978-1-63157-584-6 (e-book)

Business Expert Press Managerial Accounting Collection

Collection ISSN: 2152-7113 (print)
Collection ISSN: 2152-7121 (electronic)

Cover and interior design by Exeter Premedia Services Private Ltd., Chennai, India

First edition: 2017

10 9 8 7 6 5 4 3 2 1

Printed in the United States of America.

Abstract

It would generally be safe to assume that finance and accounting especially strategic managerial accounting (SMA) would be anathema to the software professional. This book, written from the perspective of a software professional, attempts to address that belief.

SMA is a prognostic as well as a diagnostic tool and therefore useful for making key day-to-day decisions. However the common view, especially in the IT industry, is that accounting is for the accountants, despite the fact that IT professionals are regularly confronted by financial situations such as project pricing, measuring performance, estimating risk, allocating costs, and so on. This means that every proposal needs to be vetted by the respective specialists. While this may be desirable and even necessary, the speed and reliability of the process could improve if the people who originate the proposal had knowledge of the fundamentals that go into the decision-making process.

Another distinguishing feature of the IT and services industry is their unique cost structure, quite different from the manufacturing industry on which traditional managerial accounting is based. Different categories of the industry such as software products, software development (outsourcing), online services, and IT-enabled services have their own distinct cost structure requiring different metrics. The situation is becoming further differentiated as most IT companies shift to the cloud and software ownership is replaced by licensing. These aspects are not adequately addressed by existing books on managerial accounting which are generally manufacturing centric.

The online services and mobile app industries constitute the fastest growing and most exciting segment of this industry. However there is hardly any published literature in this area for the software lay person. One chapter is entirely devoted to this subject.

This book focuses on strategic managerial accounting in context of the IT software industry, where activities are typically organized as projects which have specific goals and finite life. It seeks to equip the IT professional with some of the knowledge and skills that are generally delegated to the managerial accountants, in an attempt to assist them in making more informed decisions.

Keywords

cost allocation, cost behavior in IT industry, cost management in IT industry, cost structure, managerial accounting for strategic decision-making, managerial accounting for the software and services industry, marginal cost, nature of costs, strategic managerial accounting

Contents

Preface

All organizations are perfectly designed to get the results they are now getting. If we want different results, we must change the way we do things.

—Tom Northup

This book is an attempt to make important contributions to the existing writing on strategic managerial accounting (SMA). First, it has been written from the perspective of the information technology (IT)/software professional and hence should be not only more readable for them but also provide them with important insights for enhancing the efficacy of their strategic decision-making. Second, it acknowledges and discusses the unique cost structure of the software industry that distinguishes it from the traditional manufacturing industry on which the concepts of strategic managerial accounting are based. In these respects, this book is quite distinct from the existing SMA literature.

Software professionals generally confine themselves to their core expertise i.e. technology and tend to leave accounting to accountants. However they would do well to realize that SMA can be useful for day-to-day decision making, since they are regularly confronted with financial situations such as project pricing, measuring performance, estimating risk, allocating costs, and so on. While these matters definitely require vetting by specialists, the speed and reliability of decision-making could improve if the people who originate the proposal had knowledge of the basics that go into the process. In fact the case studies in the book discuss situations that quite a few industry managers may have encountered in their careers. In this respect this book is unique.

As mentioned before, a distinguishing feature of the software and services industry is its unique cost structure, quite different from that of the manufacturing industry. Different categories of the industry such as software products, software development (outsourcing), online services, and IT-enabled services (ITeS) have their own distinct cost structure requiring different metrics. The situation is becoming further differentiated as most software companies shift to the cloud and software ownership is replaced by licensing. These aspects are not adequately addressed by existing books on strategic managerial accounting, which are generally manufacturing centric. This book attempts to address this shortcoming as it is written from the software professional's perspective.

Within the software industry itself, cost structures differ drastically among different segments. For example, the cost structure of an online services company (an e-commerce platform for instance) is quite distinct from that of a software development services (outsourcing) company, which in turn is quite different from that of a software product company or an ITeS company. This requires that SMA principles need to be tailored to each of these categories as one size may not fit all. None of these nuances is addressed by standard books on managerial accounting owing to their focus on the manufacturing sector.

Even though the software industry is essentially a services industry (except perhaps the product companies) it differs from the standard services industries such as hospitality, health care, travel, and so on, from the SMA perspective. This is because costs do not necessarily depend on the quantity of output (think of music or movie delivery by downloads or streaming radio such as Pandora). There may be a high initial cost of development but, once developed, the replication costs are negligible, and therefore the relevance of marginal costing or incremental analysis is greatly reduced. What becomes more relevant is the need to acquire customers as quickly as possible and then to retain them so that a self-generating ecosystem is established with the participation of multiple sides of the platform—users, secondary developers (e.g., "app" developers), service providers, and so on. This does not mean that costs are not important even though industry gross margins are much higher than those for manufacturing industries. It is just that the cost focus is different because effort or man-hour cost is the single biggest element of cost. In fact, wage arbitrage has been the biggest contributor to the phenomenal growth of the software industry in countries like India, Israel, and the Philippines.

Another factor that is distinctive to the software industry (as compared to other service industries) is the concept of user-generated content and aggregation. Social media portals such as Facebook and Twitter are prime examples of the former, and platforms such as Uber (ride sharing) and Airbnb (room sharing) are examples of the latter. The cost structures of these multisided platforms are quite unlike those of other service or manufacturing industries. (Appendix 3 gives a brief introduction to multisided platforms.)

Rapid technological transformation is another distinguishing feature of the software industry. A decade ago, no one had heard of Facebook and Twitter. Myspace was formed only in 2003, became the largest social networking site by 2005, and by 2010 it had been overwhelmed by Facebook. This requires a different set of performance measurement and financial decision-making criteria, some of which are discussed in Chapter 6. Research and development (R&D) is also an area of importance. A study by McKinsey (see Chapter 7) highlights the fact that steady and incremental investments in R&D result in lower future profitability than constant reassessment and reallocation of R&D funding. This could arguably be another differentiator between the R&D environments in manufacturing and software industries: Managers in manufacturing industries are more likely to opt for steady, incremental progress in R&D, whereas software industries, operating in a more volatile and risky environment, are constrained to continuously reassess and redirect their R&D focus to stay competitive.

One more important factor for the software industry is the issue of risk. The software industry operates in an environment of volatility and uncertainty with fast-changing technology and skill-set requirements. This fact is ignored by standard financial accounting and managerial accounting reports because it is difficult to quantify it in monetary terms and is therefore consigned to management discussion or notes. For managerial accounting to be useful and relevant for the software industry in strategic decision-making, meaningful consideration of risk is essential. How can risk be factored into the working of a software company? The nature and extent of risk vary with the type of industry. For example, for the outsourcing industry, risk is only subjectively captured in the pricing in requests for proposals (RFPs), as discussed in Chapter 4 and Appendix 1. For online companies the risk may be more existential and hence underscores the importance of constant vigil for changing customer preferences and close monitoring of the direction of R&D. For product companies it may be in the form of an "innovator's dilemma" as faced by Microsoft in the Operating Systems (OS) market, where it lost the lead for mobile OS to Google's Android OS.

This book is divided into two sections—the first deals with SMA basics while the second deals with specific issues related to the software industry.

Chapter 1 discusses the principles of managerial accounting, introduces the concept of SMA and its implications.

Chapter 2 deals with costs and how they behave with respect to the software industry, while Chapter 3 discusses the methods of allocating costs so as to align them with the company's goals. Chapter 4 is the last chapter of the first section and introduces the concepts of capital budgeting for project evaluation and enterprise risk management.

Section 2 goes into specific SMA techniques for the software industry. Chapter 5 deals with measuring the performance of online companies operating in the software-as-a-service model. It goes on to discuss strategic issues such as investment decisions for such companies.

Chapter 6 deals with strategic considerations for software service (outsourcing) companies and the right metric for measuring performance. Two important and vexing issues for the software industry relate to finding the right metrics for (a) R&D and project evaluation and (b) performance evaluation and proper incentivization of personnel.

Chapter 7 deals with the complexities of evaluating R&D projects while Chapter 8 deals with the strategic issues related to individual performance evaluation.

An underlying feature of the book is the copious use of case studies depicting real-life situations in the software industry that would help the software professional to better identify the concepts being introduced. For those wishing to delve more into the topic of risk, Appendix 1 gives a detailed account of the case study discussed in Chapter 4. Appendix 2 gives a basic introduction to the concept of responsibility centers. Appendix 3 gives an introduction to the configuration of multisided platforms, which are ubiquitous in online industry. This would give a better insight to their cost and pricing structures.

This book would be useful for accountants seeking to familiarize themselves with the software industry where the cost and supply chain structure is quite distinct from that of the manufacturing industry. However, it is primarily aimed at practicing software professionals looking to gain an accounting perspective. Therefore, those with prior exposure to traditional SMA may choose to skip chapters on accounting basics, although it may be beneficial to glance through them because they look at SMA from the software industry point of view.

Note on the IT Software Industry

This book deals with strategic managerial accounting from the perspective of one segment of industry in general—the information technology (IT) software industry. However, the software industry is not a homogeneous environment that can be dealt with as one entity. The financial dynamics of a product company such as Adobe or Symantec are different from that of an online company such as Google or Facebook, which in turn are different from that of a software development services company (also referred to as outsourcing) such as Infosys or Accenture. Table N1.1 gives the cost structure of these companies, which illustrates the different cost structures of these types of industries.

As software companies often provide a mix of product and service offerings (e.g., IBM and Microsoft), they may not be easily compartmentalized in this manner. Nevertheless, the cost structures of their different product or service streams would most likely fall into one of these categories. Therefore, in this book, we have categorized our discussion into the following segments:

(a) Software product companies
(b) Online services companies
(c) Software development services (outsourcing) companies

Irrespective of this classification, the software industry is a people-dependent business. This is especially true for outsourcing companies, whose revenue depends on number of man hours (effort). Such businesses are characterized by high employee costs, high ratio of employee costs to capital costs, and limited spending on activities such as R&D.[1] However, product and online services companies are also confronted with a rapidly changing, technology-driven environment and hence have to devote considerable resources to R&D, as evident from Table N1.1.

Table N1.1 Cost structures of software companies

Cost break-up	Product company (Symantec) (%)	Outsourcing company (Accenture) (%)	Online services company (Google) (%)
Revenue	100	100	100
Cost of revenue	17	68	39
Gross margin	83	32	61
R&D expense	14	1	15
Sales and marketing expense	36	12	12
Operating Margin	16	14	24

Source: Company Financial Reports 2014.

Table N1.2 The focus areas of the different segments.

Segment	Focus
Product company	Offering feature-rich products, reliable performance, and efficient support services
Outsourcing company	Providing quality service based on on-time, within-budget delivery. Possessing skills and competencies for addressing customer needs
Online services company	Developing large user base through product appeal and quick outreach

From the strategic point of view, these segments have different areas of focus as well (Table N1.2).

In this book we will discuss how these focus areas can be monitored with a view to enhancing competitive advantage.

CHAPTER 1

Introduction to Strategic Managerial Accounting

Accountants are in the past, managers are in the present, and leaders are in the future.

—Paul Orfalea[1]

Case Study

This was the second quarter in a row that Smart Pro Inc. (SPI) was forced to issue a profit warning, this time indicating that its Q3 operating profit could fall 24 percent y/y (year on year). Within a week of the announcement, the market shaved off 6 percent from the stock value. The stock has been down 15 percent over the past six months. At the emergency board meeting convened just prior to the announcement, the board had taken the chief financial officer (CFO) to task for failing to stem the profitability decline. The CFO on the other hand reported that both the revenue targets approved by the board in the current financial year's budget had not only been met but also exceeded. The company was therefore faced with the embarrassing situation of having to pay out hefty bonuses despite falling profits.

In hindsight, the decision to set revenue and expense targets in the budget seemed to be a hasty decision, but it made a lot of sense at the time it was taken. Previously, the company had zealously pursued profitability and their better-than-average operating profits bore testimony to the success of their strategy. However, competition from low-cost "me-too" start-ups had started eroding SPI's margins and market share. There was no alternative but to go after market share.

The CFO was also painfully aware of the conversation he had had with the newly hired Managerial Accountant at the time of the budgeting exercise where he had raised the issue of strategic cost management or SCM. The company had to decide whether it wanted to be a cost leader or a differentiator, and the budgeting exercise should reflect that policy. However, his suggestions involved allocating funds for reorganizing the company's departments to better utilize resources and reduce bench costs; venturing into more value-added areas; and retraining. With margins already under pressure, the CFO was sure that a budget that reflected higher expenditure would never get past the board.

Analysis of results clearly established that the near-term weakness in margins was driven by competitive pressure in all segments, particularly from competitors from China and India. Nevertheless, SPI's market presence was intact because its volume actually improved on y/y basis. However, the Managerial Accountant's cost–benefit analysis elicited another interesting fact—if the company had fine-tuned its revenue targets with profitability goals, the cost of refusing low-cost business may have been less than the bonuses the company had to pay for achieving higher sales targets.

There was also the nagging doubt that executives were gaming the budgeting process—projecting lower targets so that they could earn larger bonuses. One indication of this fact was that due to the cyclical nature of information technology (IT) spend, the previous year had seen a 9 percent growth in IT spend. However, SPI's budget had factored only 4 percent increase over the previous year, in line with the growth trend in their past budgets.

Jim, one of the most respected members of the board had this advice for the CEO: "Look, if you go on the path of least resistance and settle for a conservative, achievable budget, you will never take risks and in the process risk missing key opportunities. You will be a lagger and eventually you will be acquired or destroyed. Don't blame your people. Question your budgeting process or better still, ditch it! Your forecasts are all wrong because you want one figure that is a target, a forecast and a resource allocation number. That will never work— there will always be other motivations and agendas that distort the number."

Managerial Accounting versus Financial Accounting

The most commonly available financial information about a commercial operation is the financial report, which is the record of the company's revenue and expense as well as assets and liabilities. While this information is of interest to financial analysts, lenders, and other external stakeholders of a company, it is of limited use to the company's managers when it comes to making financial decisions such as pricing a product or making new investments in plant and machinery. This book is meant to provide managers with an understanding of the implications of making financial decisions that have a bearing on the future profitability of the company. Furthermore, like a good detective novel, a financial report often hides more information than it reveals. It is therefore necessary to generate more comprehensive information about the company's operations that will be of help in managerial decision making. Managerial Accounting (MA) deals with this aspect. Unfortunately, while there is an abundance of literature related to the manufacturing industry, the services industry, specifically the IT industry, has largely been ignored. This book attempts to fill in this gap.

The distinction between Managerial Accounting and Financial Accounting is highlighted by The Institute of Management Accountants (IMA), which defines Managerial Accounting as:

A value-adding continuous improvement process of planning, designing, measuring and operating both financial and non-financial information systems that guides management action, motivates behavior and supports & creates the cultural values necessary to achieve an organization's strategic, tactical and operating objectives.

According to this definition, MA is responsible for information systems that have far-reaching impact on the affairs of the company. Unlike FA, neither the objective of MA (plan, design, measure, and operate financial and nonfinancial information systems) nor the expected outcome (actions and behavior aligned to the organization's objectives) is restricted to the domain of finance. It concerns the entire operations of the company. An organization entrusts the funds of the business with many individuals who have been assigned certain decision rights and have the responsibility to deliver certain results. Business funds need to be applied judiciously to acquire other resources—people, material, machines, and time; these individuals adopt various strategies to combine the resources with unique capabilities and competencies in order to optimize resource use and maximize output. The "value-adding, continuous improvement process" that it is, implies the role of MA as much broader in scope than FA. It combines financial and cost accounting, performance evaluation and analysis, planning, and decision support; it provides management with necessary tools and techniques to identify and manage internal and external risks; analyze vast amounts of data; and use them for planning, budgeting, performance evaluation, control, and decision-making.

MA has transitioned from an information processing system to a more pervasive, business solution framework for various reasons, many of which are more acutely felt in the technology industry: constant price pressure; growth pressure; cost squeeze; disruptive technology; availability of big data and data analytics tools; network economies; and above all, the impact of a volatile, uncertain, complex, and ambiguous world. It is therefore important that every manager in the software industry be equipped with the skills to use this business solution framework.

Most FA statements one comes across, such as balance sheets, profit and loss statements, and cash flow statements, are generally meant for external use, for example, for the shareholders, tax departments, creditors, and analysts. MA statements on the other hand are meant for internal use by the company's managers and are therefore catered to their specific needs. This distinction leads to important differences between FA and MA:

(a) *Standards*: As FA is primarily meant for external agencies, it is important to have consistency in reporting of financial data. For this purpose, every country has Generally Accepted Accounting Principles (GAAP) that are required to be followed when reporting financial data. MA, however, is meant for the internal use of a company, and therefore can be tailored to meet the specific needs of that company. This implies that:

   i. MA can be as detailed as required by the company's management, whereas FA only needs to comply with the applicable GAAP.

   ii. MA can include nonmonetary information such as effort hours and bandwidth usage and all information need not be converted into dollars. FA deals strictly with monetary information. In fact, due to this restriction, some companies have attempted to monetize such intangibles as employee worth and brand worth so as to include it in their financial statements.

(b) *Past versus Future*: FA reports past transactions of a company, whereas MA is forward looking and is meant as a tool for assisting in making decisions about the future of the company. Cost measurement and performance evaluation roles use historical data, whereas the planning and decision support roles are predictive.

MA is used for various objectives, for example, product costing and pricing, planning and budgeting, performance evaluation, and administrative control. Let us examine each of these objectives in more detail:

(a) *Product/Service Costing and Pricing*: It is critical for a company to accurately determine the cost of producing and selling each product because it has a direct bearing on its profitability. As we will see later in the book, there are different types of costs, some of which have to be allocated based on criteria set by the management. Therefore, determining the true cost of a product is not as straightforward as it may seem at first glance.

(b) *Decision Support*: MA supports competitive decision-making by collating, processing, and communicating required information, both financial and nonfinancial. The key assets of a commercial enterprise that impart competitive advantage to it are its Resources, Capabilities, and Competencies. The role of MA lies in providing decision support continuously and consistently to (a) optimize resource utilization, (b) build and improve efficient business processes that create unique capabilities, and (c) build core competencies in order to sustain competitive advantage. It is also critical for a company to accurately determine the cost of producing and selling each product or service because it has a direct bearing on its profitability. Therefore, determining the true cost of a product or service is not as straightforward as it may seem at first glance. For example, how would you take into account the cost of services of the staff in human resources (HR) and Finance functions who indirectly contribute to the manufacture of the product/delivery of the service?

(c) *Planning and Budgeting*: Every company prepares plans based on the expectations of their shareholders and translates them into budgets or performance targets of different departments. For example, the marketing department may break down the revenue target into subtargets based on products, regions, and sales executives; the production department may break down the revenue target into effort-hours business unit-wise or even project-wise; while the finance department may prepare cash flow and profitability targets. Even HR departments can have revenue targets based on the numbers of hours of training they have organized for employees valued at a market-based hourly rate.

(d) *Performance Evaluation*: The performance of managers and different departments/units of a company can be measured by comparing actual figures to budgeted figures. This can be used to determine the compensation of managers and controlling the operations of different units. Here too, it is important not only to set proper performance parameters but also to apply the correct metrics that will optimize operational efficiency. Setting performance-based rewards may be the most challenging job, which is in the realm of MA. In a classic Harvard Business Review (HBR) article (1993), Alfie Kohn claimed that "studies ... have conclusively shown that people who expect to receive a reward for completing a task successfully simply do not perform as well as those who expect no reward." Performance reviews are the most stressful and performance rewards the most demoralizing and yet most software companies believe that they have no choice but to go through the same year after year. In 2004, Page and Brin instituted the Founders' Award in Google Inc. for those who made significant contributions to the organization. This award is rarely given out as the idea backfired, because those who did not get the award felt overlooked.

(e) *Administrative Control*: The operations of a company require monitoring and periodic course corrections. MA reports convey up-to-date information about the company's operations, which help a company to carry out course corrections and plan future actions. Individuals tend to maximize their self-interest (such as easier jobs, higher salaries, and more perks) and control systems are required to align their interest with the organization's goal of maximizing firm value. Such control systems should help monitor and motivate the right behavior. Performance metrics, incentive schemes, career progression plans, performance review, performance audit, and surveillance and security systems are all part of the control systems. Internal accounting systems are also part of this control system.

Role of Strategic Managerial Accounting

Simmonds (1988) was the first to define Strategic Managerial Accounting (SMA) as "the provision and analysis of management accounting data about a business and its competitors which is of use in the development and monitoring of the strategy of that business." According to Innes (1998),[2] SMA is concerned with the provision of information to support the strategic decisions in the organizations. Cooper and Kaplan (1988)[3] introduced the aspect of SMA techniques using information technology to develop more refined product and service costs for assisting strategy formulation. Bromwich (1990)[4] has included "the firm's product markets and competitors' costs and cost structures" as the information that SMA needs to monitor.

The strategic aspect of MA is evident not only in IMA's definition but also from the objectives detailed earlier. Strategy aims at developing sustained competitive advantage through the most effective and efficient utilization of a company's resources. Therefore, while strategy drives financial performance, it encompasses both internal and external elements. Accordingly, SMA too covers both elements, unlike FA, which are restricted to internal factors. Lord (1996)[5] has identified the following components of SMA:

- Extension of traditional MA's internal focus to include external information about competitors.
- Relationship between the strategic position chosen by a firm and the expected emphasis on management accounting (i.e., accounting in relation to strategic positioning).
- Gaining competitive advantage by analyzing ways to decrease costs and/or enhance the differentiation of a firm's products, through exploiting linkages in the value chain and optimizing cost drivers.

As mentioned earlier, the key assets of a commercial enterprise are its Resources, Capabilities and Competencies. Resources refer to assets that a company possesses—both physical (e.g., factories, sales offices, etc.) and personnel. They can be intangible resources as well such as brand name, market reputation, technical capability, and so on. Capabilities encompass the sum total of the abilities that the company can muster to sustain its commercial viability, and competencies are those attributes or capabilities that the company possesses that are superior to those of its competitor. According to Prahalad and Gamel, it is important for companies to appreciate that the quest for competitive advantage is not only a battle for market dominance but also a fight for competence mastery. However, it is difficult for senior management to focus on each and every activity of their business and the competencies required to carry them out more efficiently than the competition; therefore, their goal should be to concentrate only on the "core competencies," that is, those capabilities that are critical to achieving sustainable competitive advantage.

SMA plays an important role in helping senior management in converting capabilities into competencies and achieving sustained competitive advantage through strategic cost management. It does this by addressing the following three cost-related issues:

1. *Nature*: The nature of costs and how they affect performance
2. *Effect*: The factors that influence costs, that is, the **cost drivers**. According to Chartered Institute of Management Accountants (CIMA), "a cost driver is any factor that causes a change in the cost of an activity."
3. *Positioning*: The relative importance of different cost vis-à-vis the company's strategic goals. This enables the company to focus on those costs that align with its competitive positioning

Nature

Chapter 2 discusses the different types of costs and how they behave. It is important to note that most cost concepts address output volume issues: cost–volume–profit analysis, marginal costing, break-even analysis, and so on are all concerned with the relationship of costs with the output of an enterprise. From the strategic point of view, this addresses only part of the problem because it ignores the entire value chain of the company. "Value chain" refers to the entire chain of linkages from raw material supplier to end user (Porter 1985).[6] For example, Houlihan[7] (1987) has studied how a major U.S. automobile manufacturer tried to save costs by implementing Just-in-Time (JIT) inventory but failed because it concentrated only on its own activities and ignored those of its suppliers. Investigations revealed that as its production scheduling was erratic it put considerable pressure on the suppliers' activity. As the value addition per automobile at the suppliers' end was more than the company's, the increase in cost for the suppliers more than offset the savings by the manufacturer.

For the software industry, the consequences of this factor can be quite dramatic. For example, Sony Corporation, pioneer and undisputed leader in the portable music industry (Walkman), was the first to introduce the digital version of the portable player in 1999 (much before the iPod) but chose to focus on the hardware and only provided cumbersome and non-intuitive software. The resulting "cost" to the end user in terms to inconvenience and difficulty in use was much more than what the company may have saved by not providing more user-friendly software. The user rejected the product. Sony's decline began shortly thereafter.

Effect

There are many factors that drive costs. Riley (1987)[8] categorized two sets of cost drivers:

(A) Structural Cost Drivers:
- Scale—activities such as production, skill development, research and development (R&D), and marketing drive costs. What should be the quantum of investment in different activities that would optimize size?
- Scope—"make-or-buy decision." What should be the extent of vertical integration?
- Experience—prior experience in implementing a task tends to make subsequent implementations more cost-efficient.

How many times has the company implemented the tasks it is performing?

- Technology—the process technologies a company uses throughout its value chain can drive costs up or down. For software companies this has relevance in terms of the technology a company utilizes in its project management process.
- Complexity—the number of products or verticals a company offers contributes to the complexity of its operations and drives costs. Choosing the right amount of complexity given the company's resources and capabilities is important for controlling costs.

(B) Executional Cost Drivers:

- Work Force Involvement—As software companies are employee driven, the commitment of employees to continuously improve the company's process is important for driving costs down.
- Total Quality Management—One of the major cost drivers for software companies is the time wasted in correcting poor code, fixing bugs, and user acceptance testing. Inculcating strong belief in quality among employees is important for keeping these costs down.
- Capacity Utilization—Bench costs are an issue with most software companies. There is need for balancing the compulsion for growth with reigning in bench costs.
- Exploitation of linkages—For software companies, particular linkages with customers and contractors are of considerable significance. Customer relationship management is an important cost driver.
- Product Configuration—Are product/service design and features aligned with the requirements of the customer?

Other executional cost drivers identified by Riley, such as Plant Layout Efficiency, are not particularly significant for the software industry. According to Shank and Govindarajan (1993)[9], structural cost drivers are not monotonically scaled with performance, that is, there are economies as well as diseconomies of scale and more is not necessarily better. They cite the example of Texas Instruments, which successfully used the learning curve phenomenon to become the lowest-cost producers of microchips that were no longer state of the art.

Positioning

This concept arises out of Porter's generic strategies[10] for competitive advantage—Cost Leadership—where you offer comparable perceived buyer value at lower price; or Product Differentiation where you offer higher perceived buyer value but at a comparable price. Differentiation incurs costs and therefore a low-cost strategy, achieved by offering relatively standardized products with features acceptable to many customers, will not carry any differentiation. This means that each of these strategic choices leads to different cost focus, as discussed by Shank and Govindarajan. For example, for a company aspiring to be a cost leader the cost of providing product features is of low importance because their targeted customer buys on considerations of price rather than features. On the other hand, the cost of providing product features is very important to a differentiator company, because it differentiates its products on the basis of superior features. Similarly, controlling marketing costs can be of critical importance for cost leaders who operate on low margins but of low importance to differentiators whose products command better margins.

For the software industry, the cost focus also depends on the category a company is in. As mentioned in the Preface, for example, an outsourcing company generally has to compete on the basis of hourly charge and hence has little scope for differentiation. In the initial stages, the general perception by U.S. clients of Indian outsourcing companies was the lack of technical capability and uncertain service standards due to lack of infrastructure and good project management capabilities for remote project implementation. Therefore, companies such as Infosys tried to differentiate themselves by projecting their "Global Delivery Model" that ensured service of high quality and that had very good success. However, very soon other Indian rivals entered the fray with their own offerings, differentiation evaporated, and the business was reduced to an hourly rate game.

The other type of software companies, that is, product companies, have a very different cost structure as we shall see in subsequent chapters. Here differentiation is a vital component for success because the goal is "platform dominance." The term refers to the fact that the utility of a software product increases as the user base expands because complementary products enter the market starting a virtuous cycle of expanding usage till the product assumes the status of an industry standard or "platform" that users and complementary product makers adopt. Therefore, the race is to gain as many users as possible in the shortest possible time frame.

A somewhat similar situation arises in the third category of software companies, that is, the online service providers. Here again the race is for platform dominance but the cost and revenue structures are different from those of product companies. Therefore, differentiation is the dominant driver for this type of companies.

The relationship between cost focus and strategic choice can be summarized as follows:

Category	Strategic choice	Critical area
Software service providers (outsourcing companies)	Cost leadership	Personnel cost Budget control
Product companies	Product differentiation	Product features Marketing cost analysis Competition analysis
Online service providers	Product differentiation	Product features Marketing cost analysis Competition analysis

Aligning Goals and Interests

As SMA reports are used for making important decisions that have a profound bearing on the company's future performance, it is vital that they represent a true and undistorted picture of the company's status. As mentioned earlier, senior management can measure or capture whatever information they wish, including nonmonetary information. However, you get only what you measure; so it is important to avoid the pitfalls of "confirmation bias," which can lead to faulty choices. Confirmation bias is the tendency to favor information that confirms one's beliefs or preconceived notions and overlook evidence that contradicts them. Simpson and Muthler (1987)[11] have documented one example of this phenomenon that brought Ford Motor Company to the brink of bankruptcy. The notion that profit is a function of manufacturing efficiency led Ford to concentrate on increasing production rather than minimizing product defects. The servicing of defective products and consequent loss of customer confidence was far more costly than any gains due to increase in factory efficiency. A similar situation can arise if a software developer, in its objective to expand rapidly, aggressively bids for large projects. Once orders start flowing in, the company scrambles to hire developers and immediately deploys them on live projects. The resulting project delays, avoidable software glitches, and ensuing customer dissatisfaction can far exceed the profits from these contracts.

Other pitfalls include incorrect allocation of fixed costs in a multiproduct company, which can distort the profitability profiles of different products, leading to the company to focus on the wrong products. Furthermore, in measuring the performance of employees, it is very important that the information generated by these reports is free from unintended bias because this has a direct bearing on the morale of the employees. For example, if the manager's performance bonus is linked to profitability but uncontrollable costs such as "administrative overhead" are ignored, the profitability picture may be distorted by increase in overheads over which the manager has no control. The different types of costs and their classification are discussed in the following chapter.

Another important goal for SMA systems is to ensure that the employees' self-interests are not in conflict with the company's goals. Employees also tend to "game" the process to their advantage. For example, budgets are both planning and control tools, so a sales executive may get performance bonus based on the extent of meeting the targets set in sales budget. However, knowledge that their rewards will be based on budget targets will motivate them to set easily achievable targets. Such self-motivated behavior can compromise organization's interest and the firm should devise its own mechanisms to align individual and firm interests. Similar alignments are required between (a) performance rewards and performance measurements and (b) performance rewards and decision rights. Rewards must relate to areas where performance is measured. For example, an individual's contribution to a team's performance may be to keep the team motivated and do trouble shooting whenever there are personality conflicts among team members. If this contribution is not measured, there will be no reward and the individual may get demotivated and leave the organization. Again, a project manager may be authorized to take decisions on training and development needs of the team members of the project. The firm should then have a mechanism to measure the outcome of such decisions and reward the performance accordingly.

Remember the case of Smart Pro Inc. at the beginning of this chapter? Do you think there is misalignment in goals and interests? As you look for answers you will hopefully realize the importance of SMA, and where FA statements, which are obviously not helping Smart Pro much, fall short from the management decision-making perspective. In the chapters that follow we will look at some of these issues pertaining to the software industry.

CHAPTER 2

Nature of Costs

Start with the end in mind.
—Stephen R. Covey (The 7 Habits of Highly Effective People)

Case Study

True Informatics (TI) is a medium-sized software development. It noticed that, of late, some of its quotes to clients were sometimes quite off the mark—either much lower or much higher than competition, the higher ones usually occurring toward the end of the financial year. They also found that once they had met or were close to their annual sales target they tended to be out priced by their competitors. Quotes were prepared by estimating number and type of development resources required, converting individual salaries to an hourly rate and then adding a flat 50 percent to cover the overheads such as rent, utilities, administrative expenses, and so on. This overhead percentage was based on the actual figure for the previous year.

TI decided to investigate this peculiar problem. It listed out all the different costs: employee costs, travel, utility costs, connectivity cost, data cost, hardware cost, software license cost, space cost (rent), administration cost (head office salaries and expenses), training cost, and bench cost (cost of idle resources). By studying the list they discovered that different costs behaved differently as the company's operations varied. For example, while the company's administration cost was based on the average of the previous year's figures, the projected current year revenue was 30 percent higher, which meant that applying this percentage uniformly to the current year would result in over-recovery of administration cost. Also, every cost did not apply uniformly across all projects—for example, travel cost for overseas business was much more than that for domestic business. Furthermore, it appeared that Accounts was using different criteria for calculating "costs"—using what they called "full costs" calculating the bid amount for a request for quotation but only contribution margin in reporting performance to top management.

Introduction

On the face of it, costs seem to be fairly obvious entities that should be easily dealt with. Cost is an intuitive word given a patina of precision by accountants who think that they can be calculated with great accuracy. However, as the case of TI shows, the nature of costs can be quite elusive, and therefore an important element for strategic managerial accounting (SMA). One important contributor to this complexity is the fact that costing, that is, the process of reckoning costs tends to change as the perspective from which it is viewed changes. Suppose a company car gets involved in an accident and it has to be written off as a cost to the company. What is the amount to be written off? The insurance company may reckon the cost based on the acquisition value of the vehicle, depreciating it as per its own norms to arrive at a particular value. Note that the rate of depreciation may vary among insurers; therefore, even from the sole perspective of an insurance company the cost estimate can vary. From the insurance company's internal perspective, the cost would be the amount paid out as insurance minus any amount received by selling the car as scrap. From the financial accounting point of view, the cost is the book value of the car. For the company that owns the car the value could be the replacement cost of the car, and so on.

> **Cost:** It is an estimated measure of the amount of resource consumed for providing a service or producing a product.

From the SMA perspective a cost is always an estimate, and it measures or should measure as accurately as possible the amount of resource consumed. Suppose you wish to calculate the cost of a software engineer assigned to a project. The most obvious cost would be his/her salary (total cost to company or CTC) but, while this is probably the one element that can be measured with some accuracy, it is not the whole story. There is the cost of providing a seat, that is, space and furniture, computer and software, utilities, facilities (gym, cafeteria—Google even provides sleeping space), and so on. Then you find that during the pendency of a particular project, about 10 percent of the employees leave; therefore, one-tenth of the cost of providing a replacement needs to be added, which means you need to estimate the recruitment and training—you get the picture! Therefore, if Accounts gives you a precise dollar figure for the cost of an employee you should know that it represents, or should represent, the best *estimate* for providing that resource.

Before going into the details of different costs it is beneficial to classify them according to the end use. A company uses costs for the following purposes:

1. Making managerial decisions—product pricing, performance appraisal of product or business units, investment decisions, portfolio analysis, and so on.
2. Determining the cost of manufacturing a product
3. Determining the cost of providing a service
4. Determining functional overheads—administrative, marketing and selling, research and development (R&D), and so on.

Managerial Decision-Making

Senior management measures performance of individuals or departments based on financial performance as well as for making decisions on investments in projects, products, and businesses. For such decisions the costs to be considered are as follows.

Controllable Costs

When measuring performance it is important to ensure that only **controllable costs**, that is, those costs that are attributable to or are under the control of the concerned unit are considered. For example, the "administrative overheads" in the TI case study are loaded on to the cost of each project. If top management decides to invest in R&D for a new application, the overhead cost increases for each project, thereby affecting their profitability. If the team lead for a project is judged by the total profitability of his/her project cost, this added burden would lead to erroneous evaluation and dissatisfaction because this added cost is not under the control of the unit head. Therefore, for the purpose of performance evaluation it is necessary to segregate **controllable** and **non-controllable costs** and only consider the former. (Question: Are bench costs, i.e. costs of unassigned programming resources, controllable costs? Ans: The answer depends on the actual situation in a company. If the company has a policy of maintaining a certain bench strength then the costs are non-controllable. However, in case of a deviation from the norm, it can be considered as a controllable cost; if the business unit decides the percentage of the bench then it is a controllable cost for that unit. It should however be borne in mind that a higher bench tally may be due to the commercial department not getting enough orders or the production department deciding to retain scarce programming talent or other company-specific issues. A proper performance evaluation plan must take these factors into consideration.)

Incremental Costs

A similar error will result if investment decisions are made based on costs not directly *relevant* to the concerned project, and all others are not ignored. These are costs that will be added if a particular investment decision is made and so they are called **incremental** or **relevant costs**. For example, a company has the alternative of either buying a license for a software product or using it over the cloud, and the comparative costs are:

	License ($)	**Cloud ($)**
Cost of software per user	100 (lump sum)	2 per month
Cost of installation	50	20
Cost of on-site maintenance	200 (over 5 years)	200
Cost of upgrade after five years	50	0

In this example, the cost of maintaining the software on site is the same for both alternatives and therefore is irrelevant. The total of other costs over a five-year period (the projected lifetime of the software) is:

Total cost for license option: $200
Total cost for cloud option: $140

Based on costing alone the cloud option is better. (Question: Is incremental costing the sole criterion for decision-making? Ans: No. In actual practice, the decision may take into account nonmonetary factors such as data security, privacy, reliability etc.)

Sunk Costs

These are costs that have been incurred by a company in the past and remain unchanged irrespective of any subsequent action or decision of a company. For example, a company decides to upgrade to a newer version of a software product and pays $100,000 for it. Later it is discovered that there is an alternative solution from another vendor that offers a totally new approach. In this situation, the amount of $100,000 spent is irrelevant to the decision of whether to go for the new solution or not—whatever solution the company opts for this outgo of money will remain the same. What is relevant is: a) the extra value the company can get from the new solution and b) the salvage value of the software purchased.

The issue of sunk costs is a difficult question for most companies. The normal instinct for management is to try and factor this cost in making future decisions because it is painful to "waste" the money spent. However, this can distort the picture and lead to suboptimal decision-making. This raises the question whether a software company should consider the development cost of a new version of software as a sunk cost. We shall discuss the pros and cons of this question later in the book. (Question: Are sunk costs included in financial statements? Ans: Yes. Sunk costs are actual costs that are accounted for in the company's books of accounts and treated as per the accounting policies followed by the company.)

Opportunity Costs

These are costs associated with choosing one of two alternatives. If the value (benefit to company) in choosing alternative A is v_1 and value of alternative B is v_2 then the opportunity cost of choosing A is v_2 and represents the value that is forgone in choosing that alternative. This implies that there is merit in choosing the alternative that has the lower opportunity cost—alternative A should be chosen only if v_2 is less than v_1. For example, consider a company working on a software project for an existing customer and sees the prospect of another project with profit potential of $50,000. However, accepting the new order will mean diverting some developers from the existing customer, resulting in delays in delivery schedules. The opportunity cost of refusing the new order is $50,000. On the other hand, if the margin from the existing customer (minus loss due to penalties and loss of reputation) is $40,000, the opportunity cost of accepting the new order is $40,000. As this is lower than the benefit from the new contract, the company would be justified in accepting the additional contract. It is important to note that this decision is based purely on monetary terms and does not take into account any intangible factors such as long-term benefits versus one-off order, the importance of either client for future business, and so on. (Question: Are opportunity costs taken into account in financial accounting? Ans: They are not considered in the profit-and-loss statement but can appear in the notes to accounts or management discussion that form part of the financial statements. Auditors sometimes qualify balance sheets by mentioning potential loss or foregone profit due to a particular management decision.)

Classification of Costs

Manufacturing a tangible product requires three types of inputs: labor, material, and manufacturing infrastructure. For the service industry it is mainly effort and infrastructure that are required. The costs associated with these inputs are as follows.

Direct Effort

In the software industry, the main input for a company, whether it is in the product or service space, is the number of hours that go into providing it. Direct effort refers to the number of hours that are directly assignable to a particular product or service. For example, the number of hours logged in by programmers in developing a piece of software constitutes the direct effort that went into its development. On the other hand, the hours of the supervisor would be indirect effort if he/she is responsible for multiple projects. Direct effort is the equivalent of direct labor for manufacturing industries. (Question: Would the effort of the project lead be direct or indirect effort?)

Direct Material

Direct material refers to material and components that go into the making of a product. As software industries deal with intangible products there is generally no direct material cost other than the cost of media (CD-ROM containing the software product) and packaging, which is negligible compared to the price of the product.

Production Overhead

For a software company this represents the cost of providing infrastructure for software development and is similar to the factory overhead for a manufacturing industry. This represents the cost of providing workstations, communication links, software licenses, servers and data centers, employee welfare (e.g., canteen), and so on. This also includes traditional costs such as depreciation and insurance. It is important to differentiate between production overhead and normal office overheads and administrative costs, because in a software company sometimes there is no clear demarcation between production center and office. (Question: Is travel cost an office overhead? Ans: Quite often members of the production team need to travel, for example, for specification gathering, technical discussions, field testing, and so on. These travel costs are part of production overhead. Travel by the marketing team or senior management or head office staff should form part of the administrative overhead.)

Costs have some other properties that can also be used to classify them:

1. *Behavior Pattern*—Do they remain fixed or do they vary with production volume?
2. *Timing of Recognition*—Do they arise when a product or service is produced (manufactured) or do they arise during a period irrespective of whether there is production or not?
3. *Relationship*—Are they directly related to an activity or only have an indirect bearing?
4. *Activity*—With which functional area are they associated?

Behavior Pattern

Fixed and Variable Costs.

In a manufacturing industry we can identify two distinct types of costs—one that varies in direct proportion to the level of production or activity, called the variable cost, and another that is essentially fixed and is not affected by the level of production or activity and hence known as the fixed cost. The relationship is depicted in Figure 2.1. An example of variable cost is the cost of raw material or components used in producing one item—it varies in proportion to the number of items produced. Fixed costs on the other hand include items such as factory rent, insurance, depreciation, and service overheads (cost of the quality control department for example). However, the picture is not so clear cut in all instances. For example, wages can be considered fixed or variable depending on the prevailing situation—in the United States, they can be variable because employees are often paid by the hour, but in India they are considered fixed because employees are generally paid fixed salaries (with possibly a variable component such as bonus or overtime) and it is difficult to let go of excess labor. In real life, it is generally a mixture of both with a fixed component comprised of permanent workers and a variable component comprised of contract labor that are paid on a "piece rate" basis.

In multiproduct companies, there is another factor of complication. While variable cost can be directly attributed to the concerned product,

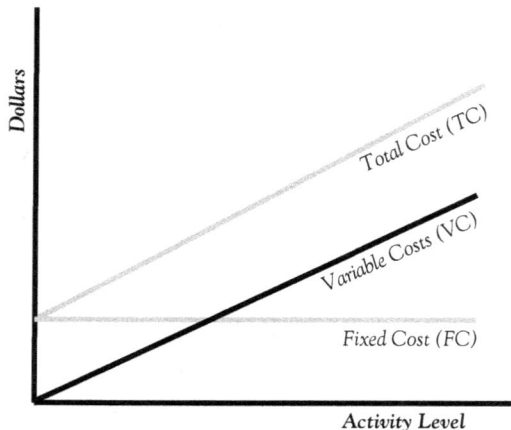

Figure 2.1 Fixed and variable costs

fixed costs are independent of the variety or quantity of products produced. Therefore, fixed costs need to be allocated to (i.e., divided among) the different products. The criterion for allocating this cost is important because it determines the total manufacturing cost of each product and therefore its profitability. There is no standard formula for allocating fixed costs and different companies have different criteria for allocating them. However, as we shall see later in the discussion on costing, no formula is perfect and the manager/decision-maker should be alert to the distortions that could arise, to prevent overburdening of some products and under-burdening of others. As a consequence, it can lead to wrong pricing of products.

As mentioned before, managerial accounting has primarily concerned itself with manufacturing companies where both fixed and variable costs constitute a finite (non-negligible) proportion of the total cost. In the information technology (IT) software industry however, variable costs for packaged software products are often negligible as compared to the fixed cost of developing a product. For example, Microsoft may spend hundreds of million in developing a new version of Windows but the per-unit cost of manufacturing it is just the cost of transferring it on to a CD or DVD, and packing it for sale is negligible. In fact, even this packaging cost is now being dispensed with because of the facility of downloading the software over the Internet. This introduces a new dimension in costing and pricing of a product.

Furthermore, all costs do not fall nicely into the fixed or variable category. For example, communication costs can be mixed or semi-variable for a dedicated data link for an overseas client if there is a minimum monthly charge and extra based on the amount of data traffic.

Timing of Recognition

Product and Period Costs

Another way of categorizing costs is by segregating them between costs that are directly assigned to manufacturing of a product, called product costs, and those that are incurred over a period unrelated to the production of goods, called period costs. Product costs are typically manufacturing costs and the two terms are used interchangeably. Period costs refer to items such as selling and marketing costs, and general and administrative costs that are incurred during the accounting period in question. While this classification is generally based on the manufacturing industry, we can also reckon cost of development resource as product cost for the software industry. Period costs are similar for both.

Relationship to Activity

Direct and Indirect Costs

Another method of classifying costs is to segregate them into those costs that are directly related to the creation of a product or service or to a specific department or unit (or a project in an IT setting); and others that are incidental to the creation process or cannot be directly attributed to a particular department or unit. As their names suggest, the former are known as direct costs while the latter are called indirect costs. The composition of this classification can vary depending on the end objective: for example, a large software company may have a portion of its technical staff unassigned to any project, that is, on the bench. If this pool of people is a general pool and not attached to a particular vertical of the company then their cost may be considered as an indirect cost. However, if one vertical, say telecom sector, has people on the bench then their cost is a direct cost for the telecom division. The same applies if one considers individual projects instead of verticals. Another example—consider a company that executes software projects both onsite as well as offsite for overseas clients. However, clients from countries such as the United States and Europe insist that all their vendors take safety insurance cover for all onsite personnel. Instead of separate insurance cover for individual programmers, the company takes blanket insurance for its staff working overseas. The cost of this insurance is a direct cost for the onsite staff, but is an indirect cost for the different projects the company is executing overseas.

In the manufacturing industry, a similar demarcation exists. For example, consider a sugar manufacturing company that has two production facilities. It sets up a procurement and transportation (P&T) department that aggregates sugarcane from the nearby areas where it is grown and quickly transports them to the crushing facility (since sugarcane has to be crushed within 16 hours of harvesting). The factories produce three types of products: packaged crystal sugar, sugar cubes, and molasses (a by-product in sugar production that is used for making alcohol). The cost of the P&T department is a direct cost for the factories but is an indirect cost for the three end products. The allocation of indirect costs is a tricky issue that may vary from company to company depending on the actual ground situation—it can be a percentage of the direct production cost of the product, or on a weight basis (per kilogram of product produced), or simply divided equally between the three products. There is the added complication that there are two factories; so a criterion is needed for splitting the total P&T cost between the two (e.g., equal split or in proportion to the weight of sugarcane used, or any other criteria considered appropriate for the company's operations).

Relationship to Functional Area

Every organization has multiple departments or functional areas such as corporate office, marketing and sales, service and maintenance, R&D (new technology development), and so on. Costs can also be classified according to the functional area, that is, administrative costs, marketing and selling costs, R&D costs, production costs, and so on. For strategic decision making, each of these costs can be further classified as fixed/variable, direct/indirect, period/product, relevant/unrelated, and controllable/non-controllable.

Relationship between Fixed and Variable Costs

This brings us to the problem highlighted in the case study at the beginning of the chapter—the problem of spreading indirect costs over the range of activities or projects of a company in a manner that truly reflects the actual total cost of an activity or project. We have seen that direct cost, manufacturing cost, and product cost are all variable costs as they are directly related to the production of a product or volume of an activity. The price at which the product or service is set should recoup this variable cost plus leave a contribution margin that equals the indirect costs and

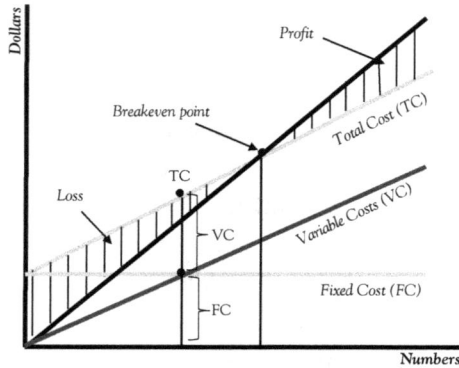

Figure 2.2 Breakeven point[1]

profit margin. This relationship can be used to determine the breakeven point, which is the quantum of sales required to exactly cover fixed costs. The margin on any sale higher than that point constitutes the profit (see Figure 2.2).

The relationship between costs and profit depicted in Figure 2.2 can be used to carry out an analysis of the interplay among costs, production/sales volume, and profit—the cost–volume–profit analysis. This is based on the following profit equation:

Profit = (Unit selling price − Unit variable cost) × Quantity sold − Total fixed cost

The difference between unit selling price and unit variable cost is also called the contribution margin per unit. The profit equation can be rewritten as:

Profit = Contribution margin per unit × Quantity sold − Total fixed costs

In such cases, it is more convenient to consider sales volume for different products rather than cost per unit. Breakeven point is the point at which the total contribution margin (unit margin × units sold) is equal to the total fixed costs. After breakeven point sales have been achieved, profit can be maximized by maximizing sales through price discounts as long as the unit contribution margin is kept positive (i.e., selling price is higher than the variable cost). Sometimes it is not feasible to consider per-unit cost due to a large and diverse variety of products as in the case of a supermarket. The equation also shows that if total fixed costs are lower, breakeven point is reached at a lower quantity of production or volume of activity. These properties can be used in what is called a cost–volume–profit analysis for optimizing profit by choosing the right product mix.

While this analysis can be used for profit maximization in a manufacturing setup, it is of little use for software industries because of the nature of fixed and variable costs and how revenue is generated. The software industry can be generally classified as being of three types based on cost structure and revenue model:

1. Software product companies (e.g., packaged software companies)
2. Online service providers (e.g., Software-as-a-Service or SaaS)
3. Software development service providers (e.g., outsourcing companies)

For a software product company, personnel costs (along with the associated infrastructure costs) go into the development of the product and as such are either investments that are capitalized or considered as sunk costs and expensed out in the year they are incurred. They are not like the fixed costs in a manufacturing company because once the product is ready, product costs (i.e., variable costs) are negligible and indirect costs are incurred mainly toward product support, administrative and marketing expenses, which are a relatively small percentage of revenue. For example, the Microsoft Business Division (which primarily sells MS Office) had a revenue of $24.72 billion in 2013 while its operating income was $16.19 billion (64.5 percent of revenue). The costs (termed as "cost of revenue") include R&D expenses and other items such as foreign currency loss, which, if excluded would raise the contribution margin close to 81 percent.[2] For "manufacturing" packaged software, both variable costs and fixed costs are low, and the difference between selling price and contribution margin is small. In this situation, breakeven point becomes less important and the focus shifts to recovering product development costs instead.

Box 2.1

The typical cost structure of software companies in the mature phase (Microsoft, Adobe, SAP) differs from that of physical product companies in the same phase (Siemens, GE, Walmart, BMW) in a significant way[*]:

	Mature Phase	
	Software	Physical Product
Cost of Revenue	25%	75%
Other Operating Expenses	50%	15%
Operating Profit	25%	10%

However for software companies in the growth phase (Facebook, LinkedIn, Salesforce.com) other operating expenses are significantly higher (60 to 80 percent), which is probably the reason for their incurring losses for a considerable period of time before revenues catch up.

[*](Hoisl Barbara (2013). Moving to a Digital Business Model—Opportunities and Challenges. www.barbarahoisl.com)

Similar costing scenarios exist for SaaS and other online service providers—the product development cost is a sunk cost and there is no concept of manufacturing here because their service is online. Here product costs include support and maintenance costs as well as server and connectivity costs. These costs not only constitute a small percentage of total revenue but also can be semi-variable depending on the operating model of the company. However, period costs, that is, sales and marketing, R&D, and general and administrative expenses can be quite high. For example, Salesforce.com, in 2013, had a total revenue of $4,071,003, with the cost of revenue being only $968,428, but their period costs were very high at $3,388,649 or 83 percent.[3] (See text box.)

For software development (outsourcing) companies, revenue is generated by the number of person-hours billed; therefore, employee costs constitute a major portion of total costs. For example, the employee costs for financial year 2013 for the Indian IT outsourcing company Infosys were 59 percent of revenue, whereas all other costs were 14 percent, leaving an operating margin of 27 percent.[4] There are no product development costs that need to be amortized or written off. Employee costs can be fixed if the resource is hired by the company, and so the emphasis is on ensuring that unutilized resources are kept to a minimum. However, they can be variable if resources are contracted from outside and paid on an hourly basis. In actual practice, it is generally a mixture of both.

It will be clear from Figure 2.2 that (a) incorrect classification of fixed and variable costs will change the cost graphs and shift the breakeven point; and (b) once breakeven point has been reached, that is, all fixed costs have been recovered, all further sales will be profitable as long as the pricing is higher than the variable cost. Thus, in the case of TI, the company discussed in the case study at the beginning, the fixed costs were fully recovered once the annual sales budget was achieved and they could price their services more aggressively after that and still be profitable. However, classification of costs into fixed and variable is not very straightforward—some are semi-variable (vary in steps) while others are mixed. Infrastructure is one example of the mixed nature of costs: for a manufacturing company, the cost of running a factory is generally considered a fixed expense; however, for a software company, the cost of office space and seats may be fixed for some time but as business expands and more seats are needed it can vary in steps. Even employee costs are generally considered as fixed but if a large number of contract programmers are hired their expense is a variable cost. It is important, therefore, to carefully identify these costs and, when making pricing decisions, take them into account appropriately in order to optimize profitability.

The problem of recovering indirect (fixed) costs becomes more complex for multiproduct companies, where they have to be apportioned to multiple products. The methodology or process of assigning indirect costs is known as cost allocation, which is discussed in greater detail in Chapter 3. Unfortunately, there is no single clear-cut norm for allocating costs—they vary from industry to industry and from company to company depending on their specific operational requirements. A typical problem is the overburdening of some products and underburdening of others, leading to a distorted profitability picture for different products or services. Let us consider some general principles. One way of addressing this problem is by **marginal costing,** where instead of considering full cost only the extra cost of providing the additional product or service is considered. In other words, we consider the contribution margin that results from the extra sale and use that to make the pricing decision.

Strategic Decision-Making

Incremental or relevant costs have been discussed earlier. An important aspect of managerial accounting is **incremental analysis** as a tool for strategic decision-making. Incremental analysis deals with the change in cost caused by an associated change in revenue—that is, the increase in costs when additional revenue is contemplated. As we shall see later in the discussion on the nature of costs, some costs such as office rent remain unchanged irrespective of the level of activity. Other costs such as expenses for contracted software developers (normally paid on hourly basis) vary in proportion to the level of activity. Consequently, total costs (fixed + variable) may not vary in direct proportion to the activity level. Therefore, strategic managers use incremental analysis for comparing the profitability of different alternatives. This involves determining the change in revenue caused by an alternative, (i.e. **incremental revenue**) and the associated change in costs, (i.e. **incremental costs**) to decide which alternative gives the highest profitability.

It is important to note that incremental analysis is just a numerical consideration of changes in cost and revenue. It is certainly not the only criterion for decision-making.

Case Study: Pridecorp LLC is a medium-sized software outsourcing company. Its skillset is in the fast-growing area of mobile apps, an expertise resulting from its relationship with Microsys Technologies, a large provider of popular mobile apps, and one of its major and most enduring customers. Pridecorp is approached by a small start-up for developing software for its product idea with huge potential in the mobile social networking space. Time to market: eight weeks. However, as the start-up is strapped for funds it has offered to pay 50 percent of

*development cost in cash and rest as 20 percent equity in its venture.
Pridecorp feels that the idea does have good potential and if it succeeds
even modestly the payoff from the 20 percent stake would be substantial. The numbers generated by the production department are:*

Estimated total effort: 1,000 hours

20 percent contingency: 200 hours (standard practice at Pridecorp)

Charge per hour: $150 per hour

*Cost of effort: $100 per hour (including standard 40 percent
overhead)*

*As Pridecorp had always wanted to enter the mobile app
space directly, this proposal presented a good opportunity. Due to a
temporary lull in orders from Microsys, Pridecorp has three mobile
app developers on the bench.*

From the managerial accounting point of view the choice is obvious because incremental analysis reveals that the incremental cost is
zero because the product can be developed by the persons in the bench.
(Q: What about the 40 percent overhead? Ans. The overhead is not a
relevant cost.) The cash portion of the payment is pure profit and the
equity stake not only presents a substantial profit potential but also gives
Pridecorp an entry into the mobile app market. However, from the strategic decision-making point of view, there are other considerations as well:
How will it affect their vital relationship with Microsys? What happens if
the product requires some enhancements and there is no bench strength?
What happens if the venture requires more funding? (Q: What other
issues can you think of?)

Operating Leverage

The interplay of fixed and variable costs provides a measure of the degree
of dependence of a company on sales of individual products (or projects
in the case of the software industry). There is a quantitative measure for
this interplay called operating leverage, which is a measure of how revenue growth affects growth in operating income. As the operating margin
is revenue minus variable costs, it represents the surplus that is available
for covering fixed costs of the company. This means that if a company

has fewer projects (sales instances) but with a high operating margin then every individual project or sale will contribute greatly to fixed cost coverage. In such a circumstance, the company is said to be highly leveraged because there can be a wide swing in sales leading to a large change in fixed-cost coverage. For example, if an outsourcing company has only a handful of large customers it is highly leveraged because the loss of one client would considerably affect its contribution margin. The degree of operating leverage (DOL) is denoted by the ratio of change in earnings before interest and taxes (EBIT) to change in sales:

$$\mathbf{DOL} = \frac{\textbf{\% Change in EBIT}}{\textbf{\% Change in sales}}$$

Cost Estimation by Software Tools

The software industry has evolved sophisticated software-based cost estimation tools that capture different costs in detail and allow in-depth analysis and scenario building. While the utility of these tools cannot be denied, it is important for the strategic manager to understand the assumptions behind these algorithms because of the elusive and varied nature of costs. Furthermore, strategic analysis requires decisions to be made not only on objective (quantitative) basis but also on subjective considerations based on factors such as importance of the client, strength of the bench, importance of entering a particular market, company's growth objectives, reputation of the company, and other competitive reasons.

It is important to bear in mind that even the objectivity of a cost estimation tool requires inputs from the cost estimator, which can be subjective. For example, estimation of effort required is not only a subject exercise but can also depend on factors such as the client's propensity to change requirements along the way, responsiveness/cooperation of the client, and so on. There is evidence from a number of studies on cost estimation that this exercise is far from objective,[5] and that these distortions can be intentional: "political behaviors that distort estimates, such as resource negotiations and image management, are perceived as common and often even necessary for stakeholders in the estimation process."[6] It has also been found that despite the availability of several cost estimation models many companies continue to depend on expert cost estimation due to a number of reasons.[7] Therefore, blind adoption of cost estimation tools can have an important impact on decision-making.

Another element of subjectivity occurs due to **learning curve** effects in an organization. As the company gains proficiency in a skill set it requires less time to carry out the same tasks. The knowledge base expands, and systems and procedures get streamlined, leading to better productivity. This can be a potent competitive tool in the hands of senior management.

CHAPTER 3

Allocation of Costs

Think cost control not cost cutting: effective cost management does not always mean finding the least expensive.

—Nathan S. Collier

Case Study

Software Limited (SL) is an information technology (IT) company based in Bangalore, India, that offers services for high-end software development. One of its marquee clients is General Manufacturing Inc. (GMI), for which it is executing a large long-term project for software development services. The CTO (Chief Technology Officer) of GMI, who is spearheading the project, has informed SL that he has $150,000 left over from his current year's IT budget. He wants to utilize this unused fund to develop another application for which there was a long-standing demand from GMI customers. He feels that this project would require the same skill sets as the main contract and wants to know whether SL is interested in this fixed-rate contract worth $150,000.

The marketing department of SL passed on this request to the production and delivery who estimate that the project would require 1,000 person-hours with a 25 percent chance of a cost overrun of 20 percent. The person-hour cost for the skill-set for the project is $95, and SL traditionally charges a flat 50 percent over this amount as infrastructure cost (information technology [IT] systems, rent, utilities, etc.). Based on these inputs, the marketing department has calculated the following figures:

Total fixed contract value: $150,000	*Gross person-hour cost: $143*
Estimated person-hours: 1,000	*Total cost: $142,500*
Cost of person-hour: $95	*Surplus/deficit: $7,500*
Infrastructure cost @ 50%: $48	

Marketing department feels that even though the margin was thin (SL's cut-off margin is 30 percent) the CTO was an important client and refusing the contract could be viewed as a rebuff. To their disappointment the accounts department sent a message saying that the deficit is actually $45,250 because marketing had not factored in the "Head Office Overhead" of 30 percent. As the head office (HO) is a cost center, its costs have to be recovered from operations, and SL, as per industry practice, had set this percentage based on the current year's budgeted revenue and HO cost figures.

Marketing pointed out that it is erroneous to burden the production cost with HO overheads because this was clearly a bonus project not included in the budget and that doing so would result in an over-recovery of the HO costs. Their stand was that only marginal costs should be considered. However, production and delivery department added another obstacle by pointing out that the risk of cost overrun had not been factored in. Their estimate for the monetary value of this risk was $7125. Furthermore, they would have to consider the cost of getting the extra manpower and the costs associated with un-utilized personnel ("bench costs") once the project was over. If these costs were included, the project would result in a loss.

While this to and fro was going on there was news that another project was nearing completion whose personnel could be deployed for this contract. There was also discussion in the marketing that not only HO overheads but also infrastructure costs should be excluded because they were largely fixed costs and should not be applied blindly across the board. The consensus in marketing was that in the very least this should be reduced to half so that only the truly variable costs are included in the total costs. Some even floated the radical idea that if people on the bench were to be used for this contract then their cost should not be added to the production cost at all, or at most it should be taken at 75 percent of actual. They also argued that cost overruns were the responsibility of production and delivery, and they should be held accountable. Asserting that marketing should not be penalized for production's inefficiency, they even went to the extent of accusing production of padding their estimate of person-hours so as to make their performance look better. If all this is taken into account, marketing contended, the actual surplus would be as high as $60,938, far exceeding the profitability norms of the company. Production contests the marketing view and says that if people are on the bench it is due to marketing's inability to get sufficient orders. As marketing performance is measured on the net surplus *while production's performance depends on on-time and within-budget delivery, it is natural that these arguments would arise.*

Should SL accept the contract? Apart from the monetary factors, are there other issues that need to be taken into account? Issues such as:

- *Importance of client*
- *Prospect of getting further business from the client*
- *Prospect of creating a track record in a new application—a factor in getting future business*
- *Are they getting valuable domain expertise by executing this project*
- *Would this have negative effect on future hourly rates*

The case of SL raises some important basic issues:

1. Allocation of fixed costs is a complex business and its blind across-the-board application can lead to distortions and even loss of profitable business.
2. Does a simple incentive program such as the one followed by SL for its marketing and production departments actually lead to maximization of shareholder value, or should it be more elaborate?
3. Efficient management of human resources and skill sets is very important for an IT company to be competitive.
4. There are risks associated with fixed-price contracts—cost and time overruns. It is important to adequately factor in these risks. Who should bear financial cost of this risk?

Let us examine these issues in more detail.

Purpose of Cost Allocation

Allocation of indirect costs serves some important purposes. First, it gives an idea of the full cost of a product or service. Full cost is variable cost plus an apportioned amount of fixed cost and the cost allocation method determines the quantum that is to be apportioned to the relevant product or service. This information can be used by management as a basis for studying the profitability of different products and appropriately focus their attention and direct resources in future. Knowing full cost is also important in "Time and Material" contracts that are common in the software industry. An accurate method of cost allocation ensures there are no hidden or uncovered costs that affect profit margins without affecting competitiveness.

Second, it provides inputs for management decision-making. Consider the training wing of the human resources (HR) department of a software company. When a business unit asks for a specific training program, the HR department uses its in-house resources to conduct the program, and the cost of conducting the program is charged to the concerned unit. However, the unit head could claim that since HR already has the resources in house it is not incurring any additional cost and hence his unit should not be charged. From the management point of view, the cost to be allocated should be the opportunity cost of using a shared company resource. Therefore, if the HR has spare resources, the additional costs would be negligible and business units should not be allocated any cost. This would encourage employee training and benefit the company. However, if HR training is fully occupied in ongoing programs then it would either have to delay other programs or hire outside trainers. In this case, the cost to be allocated would be the cost of delaying other programs or the cost of hiring outside trainers.

Third, cost allocation ensures that there is no wasteful use of shared resources. In a software company, the main constituents of indirect costs are shared resources such as office space, communication link equipment maintenance and support, HR, training, and so on. These costs need to be allocated in an equitable manner and prevent wasteful use of the resource. Consider the case in which the cost of using a dedicated communication link is divided among customer support, maintenance department, and the sales department (the two main users) on the basis of their respective dollar revenue. It may so happen that the support function, whose revenue may be less than the sales, may be allocated a smaller amount of the cost but may be using the lion's share of the resource. Furthermore, departments such as HR, which do not generate revenue, may be getting a free ride and be tempted to use this expensive resource for trivial purposes (unnecessary video calls for example).

Finally, cost allocation helps in making a "make or buy" decision. Indirect costs arise from the activities of shared services or administrative departments that are cost centers and therefore do not face any competition, which can lead to cost inefficiencies. When their costs are allocated to different departments they can compare these charges with similar outsourced services and pressure the management to reduce indirect costs.

Method of Cost Allocation

The process of allocating costs is a three-step exercise: identify the targets of allocation, that is, the "cost objectives"; list out the cost items that need to be allocated and categorize them into similar or homogeneous clusters or "cost pools"; and formulate a basis for allocating these costs equitably, that is, the "allocation base" (Figure 3.1).

Identifying Cost Objectives

Cost objectives are the targets of the cost allocation process—the entities that absorb the costs to be allocated. For software development companies, these can be different verticals (telecom, banking and finance, insurance, etc.), or large long-term clients, or even individual projects and their respective teams. For product companies these can be individual products (e.g., Microsoft Windows or Adobe Photoshop).

Determining Cost Pools

The next step is to identify the different types of indirect costs and group them into homogeneous classes. The classification is based on whether a particular class can be apportioned using the same allocation base. For example, if the allocation of certain shared services (e.g., in-house maintenance and support) can be done based on cost per hour of usage then they

Figure 3.1 Cost allocation

would constitute a cost pool. Use of office space and computer resources can be allocated based on number of seats and therefore could be another cost pool. Similarly, HR could be a cost pool and administration (head office overhead) another. Cost pools can be grouped along department lines or activity lines depending on the operations of the company.

Formulating the Allocation Base

Once cost objectives and cost pools are set it is necessary to formulate a criterion that will determine the basis of their relationship. Allocation base could be hours of usage or number of seats in a department or as a percentage of revenue or some other criterion that is specific to a company. Even though for software industries variable manufacturing cost is much higher than fixed manufacturing cost, this exercise is far from easy and if not done carefully can lead to anomalies as we saw in the True Informatics (TI) case study (Chapter 2). There are four general approaches to formulating an allocation base:

1. *Relationship between cause and effect.* According to this view, those cost objectives that cause the most cost to be incurred should be allocated the most cost. While this may work for manufacturing companies, it may not apply to software companies where indirect costs are mostly fixed and it is difficult to identify a cause-and-effect relationship between cost objectives and cost pools.

2. *Relative benefits.* This view relates the costs to the benefit derived by a cost objective—those that derive more benefit from a certain cost pool should be allocated more of the cost. This means that communication costs, for example, could be allocated on the basis of bandwidth usage. Therefore, those departments that use the most bandwidth and therefore derive the most benefit should bear the majority of the cost.

3. *Ability to bear costs.* Here the costs are allocated according to the ability of a cost objective to bear the cost burden. This means that the most profitable departments or those that have the maximum revenue get allocated most of the cost. However, this can mislead

the management in thinking that others are more profitable because they are allocated less costs.

4. *Equitable allocation.* This approach suggests that the allocation base should be fair and equitable to all cost objectives. While this is the ideal approach, it is difficult to design an allocation base that meets with this criterion.

Allocation of Shared Service Costs

Shared services such as support, datacenter maintenance, HR, and so on are cost centers whose costs have to be allocated to different revenue generating activities/products. There are some important issues to bear in mind while allocating these costs:

1. *Fixed versus variable.* Shared service costs, such as administrative costs, are fixed costs since they are independent of the extent of products or services generated/produced. Therefore, the allocation method should ensure that they do not become variable from the perspective of the revenue-generating business units. For example, in the case study given at the beginning of this chapter, SL allocated infrastructure cost and HO overhead at the rate of 50 and 30 percent of revenue. Although both these costs are fixed, in the eyes of the business units, they appear as variable costs because they vary with the revenue. This was the reason for the anomaly noticed by SL.

2. *Cost-plus basis.* It is easy to estimate the costs associated with shared services; add other overheads (cost-plus calculation) and allocate the resulting cost to the revenue centers. This raises two issues: First, there is no incentive for the shared-service units to save costs or increase efficiency; second, any increase in costs of these services would result in reducing the profitability of the revenue centers. This can be a cause of dissatisfaction for revenue centers who would see their performance adversely affected by factors unrelated to their activity.

3. *Controllable versus non-controllable.* As discussed in the previous chapter, if the performance of managers is affected by cost over

which they have no control it can become a disincentive. As shared service costs and overheads constitute non-controllable costs from the revenue center point of view such costs should be subjected to greater scrutiny before being passed on to the revenue centers. One way to address this issue is to adopt **responsibility accounting system,** which relates revenues and costs with the respective business units, departments, and individual managers who are responsible for generating the revenue as well as controlling related costs.

4. *Arbitrary allocations.* Despite all the effort that has gone into the subject on cost allocation, there is no single universal method that provides a "correct" allocation. Different methods of allocation provide solutions that have equal measure of validity and deficiency and therefore managers tend to adopt the method that shows their performance in the best light.

5. *Too few cost pools.* Software companies generally have multiple projects, verticals, or activities. Clubbing all shared service costs and overheads into a single cost pool and then allocating them based on a chosen basis (e.g., team strength, project size, etc.) can lead to distortions in determining the true profitability of different activities.

Allocating fixed costs as a percentage of or in relation to an entity such as hours of effort, revenue or person strength tends to make them appear variable. One way to mitigate this is to allocate fixed cost as a lump-sum figure so that it is delinked from the level of activity. Therefore, instead of charging off HO overheads at the rate of 30 percent of revenue TI can determine a figure (say $100,000) based on the budget.

Activity Based Costing

As we have seen from the foregoing, there is no ideal way to allocate overheads—some distortion always creeps in no matter how diligently the allocation base is formulated. Activity Based Costing or ABC attempts to address this issue by breaking down processes into individual activities, identifying the costs associated with each activity and grouping them into cost pools. Then it identifies the measures of these activities, called cost drivers, and relates the costs to these cost drivers. For example, in a software company, instead of clubbing together all "shared services," the ABC method would require breaking them into individual activities and determining the costs associated with each activity (cost pool) and then identifying the cost driver associated with the cost pool. Once this is done, the allocation is carried out based on the cost drivers consumed by each department or unit.

Case study. SL was in the process of deciding whether to accept a $150,000 fixed-value contract from their major client General Manufacturing Inc. The business unit head that had to take the final call was surprised at the large variations in cost and profitability figures projected by the different departments. There was obviously something seriously wrong with the process, so he decided to ask the company's newly recruited Management Accountant (MA) to review all the estimates and come up with a recommendation. The MA identified the following areas of discord in the costing process:

1. The "Head Office overhead" of a flat 30 percent that was being added to each proposal
2. The "Infrastructure cost" of 50 percent of person-hour cost
3. The cost of risk of overrun (20 percent higher with a 25 percent probability)
4. Factoring in "bench costs"
5. Adopting full cost versus marginal cost

It was clear that overheads themselves almost equaled the person-hour cost. It was also clear that there was no clear segregation of fixed and variable costs and therefore the process of cost allocation bordered on the arbitrary. An incorrect allocation base would seriously affect SL's competitive position. This important fact had been masked by the high profit margins that SL was generating, which enabled it to tolerate higher pricing of its services. However, with increasing competition, such high margins would soon disappear. A major reevaluation exercise was absolutely necessary. After studying the costing in detail, the MA decided that the best method to adopt would be activity-based costing and he addressed each overhead item one by one.

Overhead. *The existing method of allocating these costs was to take the previous year's actual expense; increase it by a fixed percentage (again based on the cumulative annual growth rate of the past 5 years); calculate it as the percentage of current year's budgeted sales and apply that percentage for all projects for that year. It used to be between 10 and 15 percent before the directors had decided to go public and taken on additional high-profile (and expensive) foreign-based board members. This doubled the overhead even though the line managers had no role to play in that decision. The MA, after some study, arrived at the details shown in Box 3.1.*

From Box 3.1 it is clear that:

(a) *The overhead related to fund allocation is proportional to project cost and not a fixed percentage. Furthermore, it should be reckoned in fixing the hurdle rate (see Chapter 4) and not be part of HO overhead.*

(b) *Costs related to approval of special requests (the current request falls in this category) cannot be applied to all project proposals.*

(c) *Other cost pools related to either one-off events such as budgeting or specific occasions should be allocated to the hourly rate.*

(d) *Any other cost related to HO activity (as per information available) should not be allocated to person-hour costs.*

Box 3.1

Activities attributable to operations	Associated costs	Cost driver
Providing funds	*Cost of Capital*	*Project outlay*
Approving special requests	*Executive time, process cost, infrastructure cost*	*Individual request*
Marketing assistance	*Executive time, travel cost*	*Individual instance*
Budget approval	*Executive time, process cost, infrastructure cost*	*Budget request*

Based on the above, the MA calculated that the HO overhead should not be more than $10,000 or $10 per person-hour for the project in question.

* **Infrastructure cost**. Carrying out the same analysis for this overhead the MA prepared Box 3.2.*

* From the analysis it emerged that infrastructure overheads were being dealt with in the same way as HO overheads. They were based on previous year's actuals and applied as a percentage of person-hour cost. This meant that certain projects such as overseas projects that required working evenings and nights and typically extended beyond the standard eight hours a day were being allocated more than a fair share of infrastructure overheads. The MA estimated the costs for these items as follows:*

Computer Usage: $2 per hour
Connectivity: $0.50 per hour per live seat
Space and utilities: $0.25 per hour per seat

Applying these figures to the aforementioned project he arrived at a figure of $2375 or $2.5 per person-hour (approx.) for the project.

Cost overrun. *After studying the calculations of person-hour cost the MA realized that the cost was composed of the personnel cost (salary) plus an "Overhead" of 10 percent, ostensibly to cover the costs of hiring and training.*

Box 3.2

Activities attributable to operations	Associated costs	Cost driver
Central computer usage	*Maintenance cost of computer facility*	*Usage hours*
Connectivity	*Data cost, fixed monthly charges, hardware support cost, software support cost*	*Per live seat per hour*
Space and utilities	*Energy, other utilities, real estate cost, furniture, janitorial*	*Per seat per hour*

Bench costs. *The MA found that all unassigned billable resource was transferred to a pool and the costs added to the "Bench" overheads. Every quarter the cost was consolidated and used for reckoning the allocation for the next quarter. The HR department had the responsibility of utilizing this time for training and skill development. As the cost was shared by all verticals, there was no urgency for any particular division to reduce bench costs. The MA concluded that the pooling should be done along verticals and skill sets and the costs allocated to the concerned verticals.*

Full costing versus marginal costing. *The MA was aware that one of the drawbacks of ABC was that it was more suited to estimating full costs. Another drawback was that the cost of implementing and maintaining the practice was high and increased rapidly as the number of activities increased. In his present analysis, the number of activities he had identified was relatively low, but on a company-wide exercise the activities would be many more and it could become exceedingly complex. On the other hand, the advantages were improvement in cost control and less likelihood of under-costing low-volume but complex products and over-costing simple but high-volume products. In the present case, however, marginal costing was clearly the method to be applied because the existing resources were being utilized.*

The above case is only an illustrative example and not intended to depict an exhaustive breakdown of activities of a software company for the purpose of ABC analysis. It is more a template that companies could use by adapting it to their individual circumstances and cost structure.

Activity-Based Management

Just as ABC uses activities for proper costing, Activity Based Management (ABM) is a management method that analyzes activities for improving operational efficiency and effectiveness of a company. While ABM and ABC are closely related, ABM is different as it focuses on managing activities rather than costs. Software companies are personnel-oriented—employee costs are typically 60 percent of revenue; therefore, management of this key resource, including their capabilities and competencies, is vital for the sustained competitive advantage of a company. Here ABM can be of considerable help. Furthermore, for product companies and online companies where R&D and product development constitutes a major expense, ABM can be handy for improving efficiency of these operations. For example, in the case of SL, although ABC has brought forth the anomalies in costing, there seems to be a need for analysis of the process of order acquisition and delivery—from cost and effort estimation to production, implementation, and customer acceptance. Even HO overhead that has increased from 10 to 30 percent could be justifiably studied to establish whether such a large increase in expense is justified.

ABM is a four-step exercise (Figure 3.2).

1. **Determine key activities**. The first step is to determine the important activities that have the most impact on costs. In the case of SL, the entire process of order acquisition to customer acceptance should be broken down into individual activities in order that they can be studied in detail.
2. **Identify resources**. The next step is to identify the resources used by each of the aforementioned activities.
3. **Evaluate performance**. Once the resources consumed by each activity have been identified, the next step is to evaluate the efficiency and efficacy with which these resources are being used.
4. **Evolve improvements**. After studying the efficiency with which each activity is being performed, the final step is to see how the resource utilization can be improved.

Carrying out the aforementioned exercise can lead to important breakthroughs in performance improvements. Software companies can derive considerable benefits from undertaking this exercise for improving the utilization of their employee resources and project management

Figure 3.2 Cost allocation

process. The important thing is to identify the key factors or activities that drive costs and focus on their efficiency.

As the software industry is a knowledge industry, nonfinancial parameters such as on-time project execution, responsiveness to customer, and quality of software assume significance. However, these parameters are relatively difficult to quantify in software companies. For example, tracking percentage of on-time deliveries can be an effective quantifiable measure for a manufacturer of parts, but tracking percentage of on-time project implementations would be of limited utility for a software company. Regular tracking of milestones and quickly determining and correcting the cause of delays may be a better substitute. Similarly, quality of software (code) is another factor that has a large bearing on cost but is difficult to quantify. In this respect, other nonfinancial parameters such as learning curve and experience come into play.

CHAPTER 4

Capital Budgeting and Enterprise Risk Management

It's clearly a budget. It's got a lot of numbers in it.

—George W. Bush

Introduction

Every company requires funds to operate, and as funds do not come free, the company has to source them in the least expensive manner. Funds either come from shareholders as equity or can be borrowed from banks or private lenders. In each case, the party putting up the funds expects a minimum return on its investment—banks and debt holders expect interest while shareholders expect dividends or capital appreciation. This expectation, from the company's perspective, is the cost of obtaining these funds, that is, the **cost of debt** or the **cost of equity** as the case may be. The weighted average of these two costs constitutes the **Weighted Average Cost of Capital (WACC)**. As the providers of capital have multiple choices, cost of capital represents an opportunity cost for them, because it represents the rate of return at which they would forgo other choices and make their funds available for the company. Furthermore, expectations of investors are not static; they change with the changing financial situation of the company and the changing alternatives on offer by the market. Therefore, cost of capital represents the opportunity cost "today," and any attempt to use historical cost of capital could lead to error if the market conditions have changed. If the profitability of the company is higher than that of the cost of capital, the company is said to create **Economic Value (EV)**; otherwise it is said to destroy economic value.

A rational investor evaluates any investment based on the risk associated with it—the higher the risk the greater is the return on investment desired. A rational investor is defined as an individual whose decision-making process is based on making choices that optimize the level of benefit or utility for that individual. Note that benefit is not the same as monetary profit because perceived benefit combines returns (monetary value) with risk-taking profile of the individual. Therefore, evaluation of an investment portfolio by a risk taker would differ from that of a risk-averse investor, even though they may both be rational investors. This means that a company with a higher risk would have a higher cost of capital, which in turn implies that the current cost of capital for the company represents the required rate of return for the average risk of all existing activities of the company. In actual practice, the alignment between risk and return is reflected in the market price of the debt and equity instruments of the company. In the case of debt, the risk perception about a company determines the interest rate, which is the required rate of return for lenders. In the case of equity, the return on investment is a combination of dividends and capital appreciation, and the current share price represents the current risk perception of the investor. For example, if the dividend paid out by a company is D and the share price is P then the return on investment is D/P, so if the perceived risk of the company increases in the future its share price will drop, resulting in an increase in the return (D/P will increase). More risk requires higher returns.

In general, software companies, like all high-tech enterprises, are considered high risk because of the constant need to keep pace with technological development and the difficulty in correctly reading future technological trends. Product companies are considered particularly susceptible than service companies. The most recent example of this is the battle in the operating systems (OS) market being fought between Microsoft and Google. For many decades Microsoft's DOS and Windows OS dominated the market. Apple, though a significant competitor, was never a threat, and Linux is even smaller. However, Google read the future correctly when it bet heavily on mobile OS with the result that its Android OS now enjoys a dominant market share in mobile platforms. With cloud computing being predicted as the technology of the future the market for Microsoft's desktop OS may disappear. Another example is the Indian software major Infosys, the star on the Indian stock exchange and India's second most valuable company in 2010, which fell to seventh place in 2013.[1]

Therefore, investors expect a rate of return from the company based on their perception of the risk associated with the investment, and this becomes the cost that the company has to incur for utilizing the investment. Consequently, it becomes important for the company to be able to compute this cost as accurately as possible because it not only affects its ability to raise funds but also its future share price. This cost has two components: cost of debt and cost of equity. The goal of every company is to minimize the total cost of capital by a judicial mix of debt and equity. The cost of debt is generally assumed to be the interest that is payable. Calculating the cost of equity is more complex and there are different models for estimating this cost. The most common one is the **Capital Asset Pricing Model**. However, these concepts are beyond the scope of this book.

Once funds are available to a company they have to be deployed internally in a manner that maximizes the profitability of the company, that is, they have to be allocated to different projects in the most profitable manner—an exercise called **capital budgeting.** Capital budgeting is an important component of managerial accounting and requires quantitative methods for comparing the profitability of different projects. However, before we delve into the methods of capital budgeting it is necessary to introduce another related concept—**Time Value of Money**.

Time Value of Money

It is universally known that a dollar in hand is worth more than a dollar expected in future because as time passes one dollar buys fewer and fewer goods due to inflation. There could also be a risk that you may not get the expected dollar in future, which further diminishes its future value. Therefore, in a situation where a stream of cash inflows and outflows extends into the future it is necessary to appropriately reduce or "discount" the cash flows to reflect reduction in value of future cash flows. Cash flows treated in this manner are called **discounted cash flows (DCF)**.

The vital component of DCF is the rate by which they should be discounted, known as the **discounting rate**. For calculating the discounting rate we use the concept of opportunity cost, which we introduced in Chapter 3.

If a rational investor had $100 today she has the option of investing it in a way that would enable her to get her required rate of return in future. Assuming her required rate of return to be 10% p.a. her investment would become $110 at the end of the first year (100 + 10), $121 at the end of the second year (110 + 11), and so on. At the end of the fifth year, her investment would be $161. Therefore, as a rational investor, she would be indifferent between the choice of having $100 today and $161 after five years. In other words, if the **present value (PV)** of an investment is $100 then the **future value (FV)** of that investment would be $161 if the **rate of return (r)** is 10 percent. The relationship between PV and FV is given by the following general formula:

$$FV = PV \times (1 + r)^n \tag{1}$$

Or

$$PV = \frac{FV}{(1 + r)^n} \tag{2}$$

where "n" is the number of years (or periods), and "r" is the rate of return (or discount factor)

Using Equation 2 we can calculate the PV of any future cash flow provided we know the discount factor. The same methodology can be used to calculate the net present value (NPV) of a future stream of cash flows. The following case study illustrates this technique.

Case Study: *EZ-WebSitz, an Internet start-up, has developed a software program that allows customers to build their websites themselves quickly and easily. It has spent $100,000 in developing the software and expects to generate the following cash flows from sales:*

Year 0	*Year 1*	*Year 2*	*Year 3*	*Year 4*	*Year 5*
100,000	*20,000*	*30,000*	*50,000*	*75,000*	*100,000*
(Initial Investment)					

The promoters of the company had raised the initial $100,000 investment by promising its investors a 15 percent return. However, a large Internet company has offered to buy the rights to the software for $275,000. What should EZ-WebSitz do?

The first step is to calculate the Present Values of the future cash flows to be able to compare current and future dollars. The company's promoters have raised money from investors by promising them a rate of return of 15 percent. This gives us the discount rate. Using Equation 2 we get the following figures:

	Year 1	Year 2	Year 3	Year 4	Year 5
Yearly revenues	20,000	30,000	50,000	75,000	100,000
Present values	17,391	22,684	32,876	42,881	49,718

If we add the PVs for all the years we get the PV of all cash flows over the five-year time span, which is $165,551. This means that the total worth of the project for the company is $265,551 (initial investment plus the PV of future cash flows), while the buy-out offer is for $275,000. Therefore, purely from the point of view of this **DCF** analysis, the buy-out offer is attractive. The PV can easily be calculated using standard formulas in spreadsheets such as MS Excel and Apple Numbers.

It will be evident that if the total present value of future cash flows is greater than the initial investment, then the project is worthwhile, i.e, it will give a return that is greater than the required rate of return. In other words, if the **NPV**—the present value of future cash flows minus the initial investment—is positive then the project is profitable. NPV can also be used to compare different investment alternatives with different initial investments and different cash flow streams. The alternative with the highest NPV is the most preferable. The NPV method is the simplest and most commonly used method of capital budgeting.

It is important to appreciate that NPV is a notional measure that depends on the discount rate and therefore should not be considered as an absolute figure but only used for comparison of different options. Also, the cash flows need not be inflows only but also include outflows, which take on a negative sign. Furthermore, NPV is skewed in favor of earlier cash flow because the more distant the cash flow, the less its contribution to the NPV figure. Therefore, projects that have larger inflows in the initial years will yield higher NPV than projects that start with lower (or even negative) cash flows initially but yield much bigger values in later years. In the aforementioned case, the trend of revenues gives the impression that the inflows would be much higher in later years and therefore the NPV figure may not accurately reflect the true worth of the company. Finally, NPV does not take into account nonmonetary factors such as risk, strategic considerations, intangibles, corporate goals and visions, and so on.

There are other methods of capital budgeting such as **internal rate of return (IRR) method** and **payback period**. The IRR is the discount rate at which the NPV is zero (PV = initial investment), while the payback period method calculates the time taken for inflows to equal the initial investment without discounting the inflows.

Factors Affecting Project Evaluation

We have seen that the cost of capital reflects the risk perception associated with the company. The higher the risk the more interest is sought by lenders (buyers of debt). Lenders rely on rating agencies such as Moody's and S&P, which constantly monitor past and projected future financial performance of companies and publish ratings that reflect the respective risk perception. Equity investors demand higher total return (dividend + capital appreciation) from companies having a higher risk perception and this gets reflected in the share price of the company. Within a company also different projects may carry different risks that have to be factored in while setting the required rate of return. Generally companies determine a **hurdle rate** based on the cost of capital, corporate goals, and the risk perception of a project. Only projects that yield an IRR greater than the hurdle rate are considered.

Case Study. *The stock of In-Forsys Solutions (IFS) has consistently outperformed at the stock market. However, of late, its stock was* *taking a beating at the stock market even though its financial performance was consistent. They had recently launched an initiative to move up the value chain by launching a project to develop mobile payment gateway involving an investment of $7,000,000. For this they had to postpone their plans to expand their global operations requiring an investment of $5,000,000. In making this choice they had carefully estimated the weighted average cost of capital using the historical data of the movement of their stock vis-à-vis the stock market and the interest on their debt instruments. For factoring in risk they used the risk premium associated with their industry, which was added to their WACC to set the hurdle rate of 25%. Projected cash flows are:*

Projected Cash Flow	**Year 1**	**Year 2**	**Year 3**	**Year 4**	**Year 5**
Mobile App Project	*500,000*	*750,000*	*2,000,000*	*5,000,000*	*10,000,000*
Global Expansion Project	*200,000*	*1,000,000*	*2,000,000*	*4,000,000*	*5,000,000*

Using the NPV method and the company hurdle rate, IFS determined that the NPV of the Mobile project was considerably higher than the NPV of the Expansion project. Furthermore, there were substantial intangible benefits of entering a product market as compared to the services market which was experiencing increasing competition. Therefore, they expected the stock market to reward their decision and were puzzled by the investor response.

The aforementioned case underscores the difficulties associated with financial indices such as cost of capital and hurdle rate. Despite a lot of theoretical research and analysis by academicians and practitioners, these indices remain quite subjective and care should be taken when utilizing them for important decision-making as the following analysis demonstrates.

Based on the cash flow projected by the company the following situation emerges:

Mobile App Project:
Initial investment: $7,000,000

	Year 1	Year 2	Year 3	Year 4	Year 5
Projected cash flow ($)	500,000	750,000	2,000,000	5,000,000	10,000,000
Present value of CF ($)	7,228,800				
NPV (@ discount rate 25%) ($)	228,800				

Global Expansion Project:
Initial investment: $5,000,000

	Year 1	Year 2	Year 3	Year 4	Year 5
Projected cash flow ($)	200,000	1,000,000	2,000,000	4,000,000	5,000,000
Present value of CF ($)	5,100,800				
NPV (@ discount rate 25%) ($)	100,800				

The NPV of the mobile project is clearly higher than the expansion project and therefore the company seems to be justified in choosing the former. However, the downward movement of the stock means that the investor feels the mobile project involves greater risk and uncertainty than the expansion project. There is some substance to this assessment because expanding an activity in which the company has a proven track record has a better chance of success than venturing into new areas. In addition, the investment is smaller, which further mitigates risk. If the company were to calculate the cost of capital on the reduced stock price, it would be higher. For example, if the cost increases by just 0.6 percent, the NPV of the mobile project reduces to 91,331, which makes it less preferable to the expansion project.

Another challenge facing a software company is the fact that the estimate of project cost often changes during execution due to change in requirements, as per various studies.[2] This could be due to changes in technology, better understanding of the project as it unfolds and changing market needs. This also makes it difficult to compare actual costs of a project with initial cost estimates. There may even be intentional distortion in cost estimates due to differences in perceptions of individual managers—one manager's outlook may be conservative and so she may feel that more time and effort are required for developing a module, while another one may be more aggressive in his estimates. All these factors introduce an element of uncertainty in financials of the mobile project, so the investor is justifiably worried about the additional risk that it entails for the company.

Risk Considerations in Project Evaluation

A major concern in adopting mathematical criteria in project evaluation is that these criteria ignore risks associated with each project.

Case Study. *Inforsystems—All Fingers of The Hand Are Not Equal!*

Ramakrishnan, vice president (Government Business) at Inforsystems, felt a sense of satisfaction as he put the finishing touch to his proposal for fresh capital investment for bidding for a new and very large government project. Ramki, as he was known to his colleagues, was sure that his proposal would be accepted by the management. After all his division was the most important of the three divisions of Inforsystems, responsible for more than half the company's total revenue. This project would tilt the balance even further. No one would dare to question his proposal, not even the finance department. It was too large a project to reject.

Inforsystems was a 10-year-old publicly listed software services company that had ridden the outsourcing boom of the last decade. The tumultuous growth in the early years had forced the company to focus more on sales rather than financial strength. None was more acutely aware of this serious problem than Padmanabhan (Paddy), the veteran chief financial officer (CFO). He was eager to bring in fresh professional thinking in his department and had recently hired Suresh Chopra as a manager in his department. Suresh was a young MBA with finance specialization, and in his previous company he successfully implemented a system of evaluating projects based on a differential hurdle rate that took into account risk as well as the return. The implementation of the new system had caused a lot of uproar and unpleasantness that it eventually led to his resignation.

At his Business School, Suresh had learned about the concept of cost of capital and decided to calculate the company's WACC. After going through all the past and present financial statements and reading the assessments of different financial analysts and investment bankers, he estimated the company's WACC as 14 percent. Paddy confirmed that the company was indeed using 14 percent as the hurdle rate for evaluating all fresh project proposals.

A muted "ping" from his computer alerted Suresh that there was a new e-mail in his inbox. He looked at the sender's name and sighed— it was Ramki's investment proposal. Suresh had already received investment proposals from the company's other two divisions—Large Accounts division and Small Accounts division. He knew about Ramki's clout with the top management, given the importance of government business for the company. This division had shown steady growth of late, accounting for 53 percent of the company's business and therefore the major chunk of profits. However, as government business consisted of large projects and took fairly long to materialize, there was considerable volatility in the business that impacted the company's overall sales and profit projections. Furthermore, payments were erratic and often delayed due to bureaucratic red tape, and the uncertainty of business meant that the company had to maintain a sizeable bench strength. Suresh wondered how this hidden cost was allocated across divisions. The other two divisions—Small Accounts and Large Accounts—that equally made up the other half of the revenue were far less volatile but gave lower profits as well because most of the contracts were long-term relationships with the customer.

After some more calculations, Suresh was ready with his recommendations—using the standard hurdle rate, Ramki's proposal was by far the most favorable. However, if one took into account the risk due to the volatility of government business the exact opposite was true. With a sense of uneasiness, he picked up the phone to call his boss. He knew the meeting with the division heads would not be very pleasant.

A complete version of the aforementioned case is given in Appendix 1 for those who would like to carry out Suresh's analysis.

The application of a standard hurdle rate for all projects without considering the associated risk may lead to suboptimal rate of return. Riskier projects should earn a higher rate of return to account for the risk. Therefore, using a standard hurdle rate may make the company seem more competitive in projects that are riskier. Furthermore, the company is using its cost of capital as its hurdle rate, which means that risk is being ignored altogether. Over time, the company's portfolio would be skewed toward risky projects as is the case for *Inforsystems* above, where more than half of their portfolio is composed of government projects, which are riskier than the other projects. As profitability of software companies is generally high (see Chapter 3) this aspect gets overlooked and risk gets hidden. However, it can be used for strategic purposes as discussed in the last section of this chapter.

Behavioral Issues in Capital Budgeting

There is often an inherent conflict that employees face when deciding what is best for the company and what is in their personal interest. In the aforementioned case study Ramki's performance is based on the sales performance of his division. From his personal perspective the lower the hurdle rate the better it is for him because it allows his division to compete more aggressively on price. Therefore, he would be incentivized to maximize his sales and tend to underestimate the risk factor. That is probably the reason the company gets more than half of its sales from government sales. From the company's view, however, it would be preferable to forego a project unless it earned the appropriate rate of return based on the NPV method.

Gervais cites several studies[3] that show that individuals over a wide spectrum of occupations (managers, entrepreneurs, negotiators, etc.) tend to overestimate their knowledge and information. He cites several factors that may explain why managers can be overconfident even in the capital budgeting context:

1. Capital budgeting decisions can be complex because they not only require estimation of future cash flows in uncertain conditions but

also of factors that can affect indices such as the discounting rate, customer expectations, technology change, and so on. People tend to be overconfident when tackling such uncertainties.

2. Capital budgeting decisions are not well suited for learning. Learning occurs "when closely similar problems are frequently encountered, especially if the outcomes of decisions are quickly known and provide unequivocal feedback." However, major investment proposals can be infrequent and outcomes spread over a long period, which may adversely affect the accuracy of feedback and evaluation. In the software industry, every big request for proposal (RFP) is tantamount to a capital budgeting exercise, but "managers often have difficulty rejecting the notion that every situation is new in important ways, allowing them to ignore feedback from past decisions altogether." Under these circumstances, "learning from experience is quite unlikely."[4]

3. Gervais notes that "unsuccessful managers are less likely to retain their jobs and be promoted. Those who succeed may become overconfident because of a self-attribution bias. Most people overestimate the degree to which they are responsible for their own success. He goes on to note that "this self-attribution bias causes successful managers to become overconfident."

4. There is a selection bias that makes managers more overconfident and optimistic about their prospects than the general population because managers with these attributes are more likely to be hired. According to one study,[5] overconfident individuals are more likely to have generated extremely good outcomes in the past and consequently employees with these traits are more likely to percolate to the top. Furthermore, companies find that overconfident managers may simply be easier to motivate than their rational counterparts and so hiring them is more appealing.[6]

A hint of this overconfidence can probably be discerned from Ramki's attitude in the *Inforsystems* case. This behavioral trait impacts software companies differently depending on their type. For software development services companies (such as *Inforsystems*), with employee costs constituting 55 to 60 percent of revenue, this behavior can lead to overoptimistic estimates of effort involved, which can negatively affect margins. For software product companies, this can lead to delays in product development and taking up projects that may not be economically advisable. For online companies it may affect the viability of their project.

Profit margins in the range of 25 to 30 percent tend to mask risk considerations for software companies. Therefore, they tend to focus more on enterprise risk management rather than risk-adjusted rates of return. Furthermore, properly quantifying risk can be a tricky issue. For example, in the *Inforsystems* case, it is easy to quantify volatility by calculating standard deviation, and the coefficient of variation,[7] which may provide a good sense of relative risk. However, determining an accurate quantitative measure of risk that can be used to adjust required rates of return of different projects is not very straightforward. Therefore, some amount of subjective input may be required in aligning the required rates of return to the risk perception.

Strategic Cost Management and Capital Budgeting

While quantum of investment and projected cash flows are important determinants in capital budgeting decision-making, managers are sometimes confronted with situations that may require overriding verdict thrown up by number crunching. Opportunity of breaking through into new markets or verticals, acquiring a new skill set or developing competitive advantage over rivals, and other strategic considerations often enter the picture: strategic choice and competitive advantage? Does the project align with the company's strategic choice of cost leader or differentiator? Does it contribute to enhancing the company's competitive advantage? If the answers are positive then the project can be selected. This does pose the question as to how much monetary value can one attach to these nonfinancial parameters. If the project has negative NPV but is positive with respect to strategic choice and competitive advantage, what should tilt the balance? The matter has been studied from the point of view of new technology adoption by manufacturing/service units where the suggested approaches have ranged from "adopt new technology at any cost" to more structured approaches such as Refined NPV[8] and strategic-financial analysis.[9] From the software companies' point of view, some objectivity can be introduced in capital budgeting decisions by estimating a value for the strategic and competitive advantage considerations and comparing that with the NPV of the project. However, value estimations can be subject to biases and self-interests and therefore detailed justification and independent review of the estimation are a must.

CHAPTER 5

Performance Metrics for High Growth Software Service Companies

Most measurements of performance are geared to the needs of 20th-century manufacturing companies. Times have changed. Metrics must change as well.

—Lowell L. Bryan[1]

Case Study

On March 13, 2014, a news report in Bloomberg Business[2] headlined "Infosys Plunges After Murthy's Sales Growth Outlook" stated:

Infosys Ltd. plunged the most in 11 months after Chairman N.R. Narayana Murthy told investors annual sales growth may be at the lower end of its projections and lag behind industry forecast. "We are not very happy with our performance over the last two years," Murthy said at an investors meet organized by Barclays Plc in Bangalore yesterday. "The second matter of concern for us has been the coming down of our operating margin."

Shares of India's second-biggest software exporter slumped 8.5 percent to 3,357.60 rupees in Mumbai today, the biggest loss since April 12 and lowest level since Dec. 9. …. This was the second quarter in a row that Smart Pro Inc. (SPI) was forced to issue a profit warning, this time indicating that its Q3 operating profit could fall 24 percent y/y (year on year).

It was a remarkable commentary on the poster boy of the Indian software industry, which had mesmerized the Indian stock markets for the first decade of this century, reporting record profit and revenue growth and outperforming its rivals. Murthy's lament was due to a decline of 77 per cent in the rate of growth during March 2011 to March 2013, and fall in operating margin from a norm of 41.5 to 23.5 percent (a drop of approximately 45 percent).[3] *The previous year, a worried Board of the company had replaced the chief executive officer (CEO) and brought back Murthy, one of the cofounders of Infosys who served as its first chairman and CEO, and had laid the foundation for its spectacular growth in the early years. Unfortunately, the move did not seem to be yielding results.*

On the other side of the world an analyst's report datelined October 29, 2015,[4] *stated:*

IBM (NYSE:IBM) has been beat up over the last several years. Revenue has declined in 14 consecutive quarters, and the stock price has lost a third of its value. Media pundits decry things like "IBM missed the cloud opportunity," and "it's a dinosaur kept alive with financial engineering."

Despite this comment it went on to list the reasons why investors should not shun IBM stock.

At the other end of the spectrum, Accenture's Chairman and CEO Pierre Nanterme made these opening remarks at their 2015 earnings conference call with analysts:

For the full year, we delivered strong new bookings, generated record revenues, grew EPS faster than revenues, and generated strong free cash flow, all while continuing to invest in our business and delivering significant value for clients and shareholders … [and] it's noteworthy that we closed 11 acquisitions in the quarter, giving us 18 acquisitions for the full year, with invested capital of $800 million, providing us with scale and capabilities in key growth areas.[5]

Introduction

The cost of goods sold (CoGS) for a software service industry is essentially people, and company performance depends on what skills these people have and how they are deployed. Service companies, including technology/software service companies (SSCs), spend considerable energy in maintaining revenue growth and keeping costs under control. Therefore, under normal circumstances, an SSC should be able to sustain if not grow its profitability. However, as Figure 5.1 shows, despite steadily rising revenues, the CoGS for Infosys (as a percentage of revenue) steadily rose, leading to the remarks of its Chairman Murthy and hammering of its stock price in 2014.[6] The situation of IBM[7] is similar though its revenues have fallen due to divestment of unprofitable businesses.

Despite the negative stock market reaction, Infosys has been and continues to be a blue chip company and IBM, apart from being blue chip, also occupies a preeminent place among information technology (IT) companies. Both continue to generate considerable amounts of cash and are comfortably profitable. In fact, IBM has decided to return the excess cash to its shareholders, thereby turning into one of "the most voracious share repurchasers among U.S. companies" and by mid-2014

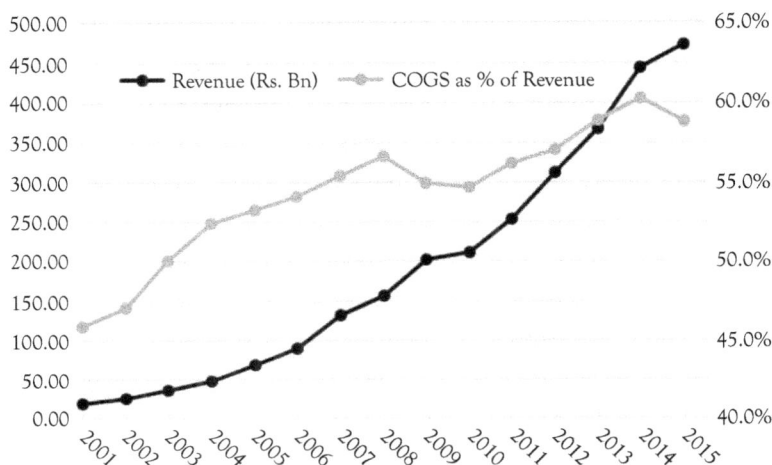

Figure 5.1 Infosys financial performance

its shares outstanding count fell below one billion for the first time in 15 years.[8]

How is it that these blue chip companies are facing such adversity at the stock market despite the fact that they continue to be profitable? Let us examine this issue from the strategic managerial accounting (SMA) perspective.

Identifying the Right Parameters

There are two levers driving competitive advantage:

(a) Increasing perceived value and
(b) Decreasing cost to serve.

As the stock market focuses only on one metric—profitability—SSCs get drawn into this relentless quest for improving or maintaining this parameter by aiming to decrease the cost to serve. While profitability is a good measure of the past and present financial health of the company, it is a poor indicator of the future. This is especially relevant for SSCs where CoGS is primarily employee cost and it tends to increase over time necessitating ever higher profit growth, as shown in Figure 5.1. This is true for most service industries in general because they are manpower dependent. For SSCs, this manpower dependency means that the pursuit of higher revenue requires higher billed hours, which in turn requires (among other things)[9] more manpower, which leads to increase in costs and pressure on profitability. However, one cannot continue to increase revenue and maintain profitability indefinitely because of the threat of entry by new players and increasing commoditization of standard skill sets (e.g., lower-level programmers).

Therefore, decreasing cost to serve may not be feasible or sufficient to retain competitive advantage over the long term. It is also necessary to increase the size of the value pie. How can this be done? In any service industry customer-perceived value depends on:

1. The ability to accurately understand the requirement of the customer
2. The ability to offer an effective and efficient solution to the problem
3. The expertise to deliver the solution in time and within budget

Understanding what the customer really wants is not as straight-forward as it looks. In real life, building an accurate customer requirement becomes difficult because of multiple agencies involved—in-house IT departments, consultants, contractors, and service providers. More importantly, the customer is generally not a single entity but a group or department that is often not able to precisely define its requirements either due to multiple (and perhaps conflicting) decision points, or incomplete knowledge of what is possible given the constraints of technology. Figure 5.2,[10] floating around from the 1960s in different versions, aptly illustrates the point.

Often the customer needs are misunderstood to be requirement gathering, that is, collection of client stipulations by technical and domain experts. This presupposes that the problem has already been identified. However, the key to strong customer relationship, however, lies in entering the picture well before that. This can only happen if the SSC is able to convincingly assert, "I know *your* industry" and "*this* is your problem" and finally "*this* is your solution." This requires three key competencies:

- Domain expertise ("I understand *your* industry")—knowledge of the best practices of the industry and the ability to look at issues in a holistic manner
- Understanding customer need ("*this* is your problem")—skill to diagnose the needs to be addressed
- Technical expertise ("*this* is the solution")—the ability to prescribe an effective and efficient solution to address the needs

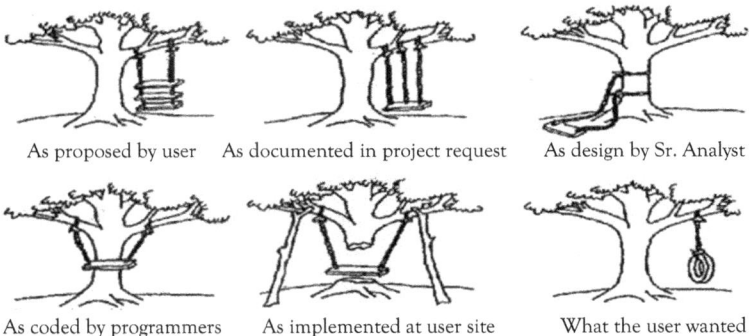

As proposed by user   As documented in project request   As design by Sr. Analyst

As coded by programmers   As implemented at user site   What the user wanted

Figure 5.2 Pitfalls in customer requirement gathering

Once this is done, the only thing that remains is implementation of the solution, and that is where requirement gathering comes into picture. If the burden of the first three steps is left to the customer and the SSC enters only at the implementation phase then it considerably reduces its value proposition to the customer and exposes itself to pressure on profitability.

This in no way diminishes the importance of implementation. In fact, the initial surge of outsourcing happened when offshore companies were able to demonstrate their ability to achieve good-quality (painless) implementation on time and within budget. But successful implementation is a process-driven activity, achievable through adoption of best practices and operational efficiencies. Therefore, over time, its usefulness as a differentiation tool diminishes as rival companies gain experience and improve their processes. The three key competencies on the other hand are skill driven and therefore can be honed into drivers of competitive advantage. Good implementation is achieved by instituting good internal processes for better execution. Key competencies are achieved by attracting the right talent. Unfortunately, top-level consultants are a scare and expensive, while the implementation level is becoming increasingly commoditized.

Competitive advantage depends on the extent to which the company's high-end consultants are able to offer the comfort to the customer that they can offer the right solution for their needs, that is, they can help the customer improve his or her competitive advantage. Therefore, Managing Client perception is vital, and for that, from the management accounting perspective, it is important to apply the right metric.

Finding the Right Metric

Pricing is a key element of any competitive strategy that places considerable emphasis on cost control. In the software service industry, employee costs are typically 55 percent of revenue and they constitute the bulk of expenditure; therefore, monitoring employee costs is an important metric. However, this is not a useful metric for cross-company comparison, except when viewed as a percentage of revenue. Even as a percentage of revenue it is of limited value because of wide disparities in overall skill levels across employees and wage differences in different geographies. For example, Accenture with a CoGS of 68 percent is not necessarily less competitive as compared with Infosys whose CoGS is 59 percent.[11] However, some other metrics can lead to better insights into the workings of different companies in the software services space.

Let us compare the three companies mentioned in the case study, which have different corporate history and DNA: Infosys, Accenture, and IBM. The revenue and CoGS relationship for Accenture shown in Figure 5.3 is similar to that of Infosys shown in Figure 5.1. While revenue continues to grow, CoGS as percentage of revenue stabilizes. The situation for IBM is essentially the same with CoGS stabilizing at around 50 percent.[12] For all three companies, revenues have grown and profitability is good as is evident from their financial statements. What is not immediately clear is their competitive situation. Therefore, from the competitive advantage point of view, the amount of managerial accounting information to be gleaned from this metric (CoGS as percentage of revenue) is limited. However, as we saw in the case study, the market perception of these companies is a mixed bag. What is also interesting is the divergence of strategies adopted by them. IBM has gone for the traditional time-tested strategy of divesting unprofitable businesses to improve profitability, and buying back equity shores up market price. Accenture, on the other hand, adopted a totally contrarian

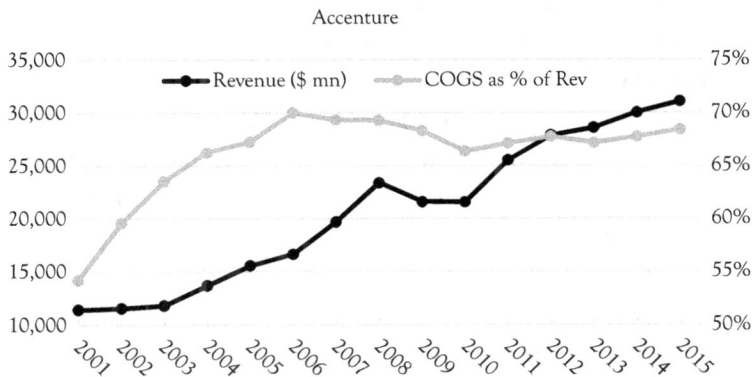

Figure 5.3 Accenture financial performance

strategy by which they embarked on a hectic acquisition drive, which culminated in about 45 acquisitions worth $3.5 billion in the last three years alone.[13] Infosys, being a conservative company focused on organic growth, avoided the acquisition route, which paid dividends initially when the growth was very rapid but faltered as growth slowed. So they went for change in senior management by first bringing back their original cofounder and chairman and then appointing, for the first time in its history, a CEO who is neither a company insider nor one of the original founders.

Let us examine these diverse strategies using a different metric— revenue per employee or revenue per capita (RPC). We have already seen that service companies are employee dependent; hence, bringing employee count into the picture provides a better yardstick for comparison. Figure 5.4 gives the revenue per employee for the three companies. Figures for Infosys are in Indian rupees, the currency in which they report their financials, while the other two are in U.S. dollars. The idea is to show trends without discrepancies due to currency conversion.

A managerial accountant can draw a wealth of strategic information from this metric. For example:

(a) The RPC of Infosys (converted into US$) is much lower than that for IBM and Accenture. In other words, the customer-perceived value for services from Accenture and IBM is much higher, which is not surprising because the Infosys business model had been based on the wage arbitrage between Indian developers and their Western counterparts.

(b) The RPC for Infosys is trending up while that for the other two is decreasing. Initially, Infosys used its cost advantage to aggressively go after market share by competitively pricing its services. As it gained experience and customer recognition it was able to improve its operational efficiencies and also tried to move up in the value chain. For Accenture and IBM, on the other hand, competition from companies like Infosys has not only put pressure on pricing but has also led to drop in RPC.

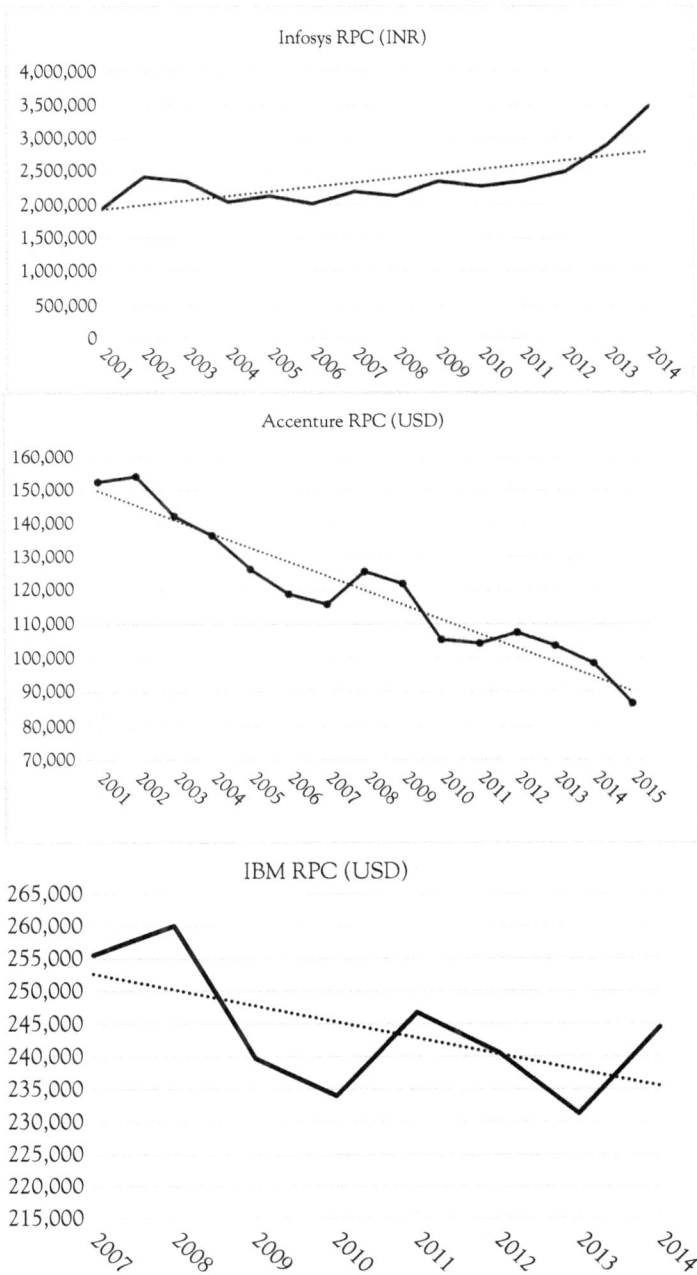

Figure 5.4 *Revenue per capita—Infosys, Accenture, and IBM*

(c) The RPC for different players will converge in the future and therefore new strategies would be required for sustained competitive advantage. This is an important insight for determining future strategy.

Conducting standard financial analysis based on company annual reports does provide valuable information about the company's financial health. However, as with most financial analyses, it is backward looking and presents limited utility in providing strategic guidance. However, if we compare per capita figures, a different picture emerges, which provides a better insight into the competitive position of the company. RPC is the most important such metric for a service industry because it reflects:

(a) The quality of employees—better qualified and more skilled person-nel enable better value realization by increasing the value pie
(b) The level of understanding of the client needs—this gives the ability to provide good quality solutions for the customer needs.

Commanding a premium is possible only if the top layer of the SSC is of a high caliber because only then a better and effective solution to the problem can be developed. The capability graph of an SSC resembles a pyramid, with the base representing the lower-skilled workforce and the top representing the "high-end consultants," that is, those whose com-petencies would provide greater perceived value to the customer. The aim should be to prevent the pyramid becoming flatter as this would represent a larger proportion of low end consultants and consequently a lower RPC (Accenture gets about 30 percent of its revenue from high-end consulting because of which their RPC is almost three times that of Infosys). Therefore, RPC is an important metric for SSCs because it reflects employee capability and therefore degree of competitiveness and future profitability.

When viewed from this perspective, the strategy of Accenture becomes more comprehensible. They first identified growth areas in the industry and then aggressively went for acquiring competencies in those areas by acquiring companies that operated in those niches. Therefore, they were able to quickly expand their competency horizon, which gave them entry into newer technologies such as cloud computing and analytics, thereby considerably improving the customer-perceived value. In the process they also acquired more high-end consultants and narrowed their capability pyramid, which will conceivably slow down or arrest the decline in their RPC, as they continue to post excellent financial results. Not surprisingly, their efforts have been viewed very positively by the stock market. Infosys has tried the organic growth with modest gains and IBM, which has rich competencies (it has the highest RPC among the three), has suffered by channeling them in the right direction (e.g., it has been late in shifting focus to cloud computing).

The per capita metric can be extended to other parameters as well, for example, per capita expenditure, profit, EBIT(Earnings Before Interest and Tax), CAPEX (Capital Expenditure), and so on, which can give important information for managerial decision-making as it allows inter-company comparison in terms of operational efficiency, financial resource deployment, employee productivity, and so on. For example, we can get insights such as Infosys has the highest per capita EBIT while Tata Consulting Service (TCS) has the lowest operating cost among offshore vendors and HCL Technologies (HCLT) has been improving its RPC.

Other Key Performance Indicators

RPC clubs the output of all employees of a company, including those in staff functions such as finance and accounts, administration, and human resources (HR). It can be further refined by tracking revenue per billable consultant (RBC), which is an indicator of the level of skill sets available in the company as well as customer perception of the value of its services. However, RBC has to be reckoned along with cost per employee (CPE) because a high CPE can offset the gains of high RBC. A healthy ratio of RBC to CPE is between 3 and 4. Similarly, billable utilization (BU) gives a measure of the bench strength and average project overrun (APO) gives the efficiency of execution of projects. A steady increase in the first three (RPC, RBC, and BU) and a decline in APO indicates a healthy company and ensures profit growth.

Service Performance Insight (SPI Research) has listed five key performance indicators (KPIs) that have a direct bearing on earnings of service companies that include RPC, RBC, BU, APO, as well as Project Margin.

Financial performance can be improved by continuously improving these KPIs through "better focus, alignment, communication and collaboration" within the company. By doing so, they advance through five levels of financial "maturity" from "initiated" to "optimized." As companies attain higher levels of maturity by "better aligning their people, processes, and systems" their financial performance improves.[14]

Effective client perception management is the key to competitive advantage and **repeat business measured by incremental revenue** from client is a good indicator of that. Therefore, effective project management to ensure implementation on time and within budget is essential and can be done by **project-wise tracking** of stage, milestones, over/under-budget situation. In effort data collection and data mining can play a critical role in good monitoring. However, all projects do not represent the same **level of criticality** to the client (or the company) and therefore it is imperative to institute MA processes for identifying these projects and having them monitored by top-level executives. On the other hand, there has to be an optimum allocation of company resources, which means that the company's attention should be matched not only to the size of the business and its profit potential but also to the size of the client (due to business potential).

Performance evaluation is another managerial objective that requires realistic measurement of employee output. At the bottom of the pyramid, remuneration may be fixed and based on industry norms and company policy. At higher levels, it may be necessary to have a variable element in compensation. However, this leads to complications due to uncertainty whether the incentive should be based on performance at the project level, vertical level, or company level. Furthermore, arriving at a fair and equitable incentive compensation for personnel engaged in delivery (i.e., coders) is difficult. This is discussed in more detail in chapter 8.

Conclusion

Managing customer value perception is an important determinant of competitive advantage. With the advent of the Internet and its explosive growth the software scenario is changing rapidly and innovation is posing constantly shifting demands for skills and competencies. Monitoring and comparing per-employee metrics, especially RPC, provides a better glimpse of the underlying changes in the industry, and therefore is a good indicator of competitive advantage for SSCs. The challenge is to quickly identify areas of growth and rapidly move into those areas, either by inorganic growth or through timely policy shifts.

CHAPTER 6

Tracking and Measuring Innovation

The story of innovation has not changed. It has always been a small team of people who have a new idea, typically not understood by people around them and their executives.

—Eric Schmidt,[1] Chairman, Google

There's no doubt: measuring "innovation" is a fuzzy business. Part of the problem is there isn't a clear consensus on what marks an innovative company.

—Scott Anthony,[2] Innovation Consultant

Introduction

The traditional view is that innovation is a disorganized and random process that cannot be measured. After all, how can one assign a value to the creativity of a person? According to one innovation consultant, even though innovation is one of the key factors of success, it is managed with the least discipline, and serendipity rather than rigor and discipline of metrics seems to be the rule. "Without a focus on product development metrics, we could be wasting a lot of time on projects of no value."[3]

But innovation is the lifeblood of software companies. It is not only the source of new products and services but also vital for ongoing sales and customer relationships through software patches and upgrades. Not surprisingly, in most software companies, research and development (R&D) departments wield greater power than the traditionally powerful departments such as sales and marketing. This is more evident in companies considered more "innovative" than in others.[4] R&D departments are no longer the isolated laboratories of the past but are increasingly being exposed to market pressures. This further underscores the importance of efficient management of R&D.

Innovation is indeed fuzzy business, and therefore it is far more difficult to measure innovation than it is to measure productivity and performance in a manufacturing setup. Even the advertising budget, long considered opaque and whose performance was difficult to measure, is now yielding to closer scrutiny thanks to modern digital technology. Measuring the effectiveness or efficiency of any entity requires that there be an input and an output, and taking a ratio of the two. For this both should be measurable. For R&D activity however, while input is fairly straightforward to measure (in terms of dollars spent), there are few clues on how to measure output. There is no flow of tangible goods or services, only a collection of ideas and concepts that do not lend themselves to quantitative analysis. Furthermore, the lack of repetitive tasks renders efficiency measurements ineffective, and to make matters worse, there seems to be a little correlation between R&D spending and success measured a growth in revenue. A plot of percentage of revenue growth against R&D spend (as a percentage of revenue) (Figure 6.1) for SaaS (Software as a Service) companies with more than $100 million revenue brings out the weak correlation. The numbers show a large variance from 3 to 37.5 percent.

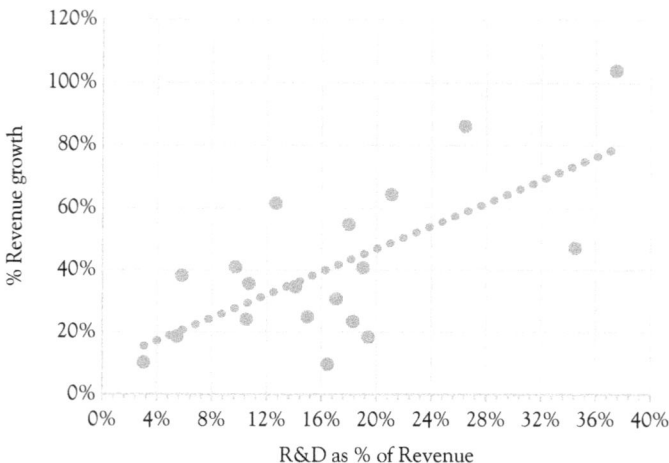

Figure 6.1 R&D relative to revenue growth

Therefore, it is clear that the key is not the amount of money that is spent but the way it is spent. Not all ideas are good and putting money into bad ideas is just as harmful as ignoring good ones.

Therefore, the important point is the effectiveness of the R&D spend rather than its magnitude. Microsoft may be spending billions of dollars in R&D (2013: $10.4 billion; percentage of revenue: 13.4 percent), so is Oracle (12 percent). But are they more innovative than, for example, Samsung (2013: $13.4 billion; percentage of revenue: 6.4 percent), which brings many more new products annually; or Google (2013: $8 billion; percentage of revenue: 13.2 percent), which is considered to be a fountainhead of innovative products? Apple, despite its iconic products, is known to be frugal on R&D—after peaking at 8 percent of revenue in 2001 (iPod launch), R&D funding has hovered around 3 percent of sales for nearly a decade.[5] That is why Apple's 3 percent R&D budget (as percentage of revenue) is probably better spent than Microsoft's 13 percent or Oracle's 12 percent. The question therefore is how to value innovation.

A study by McKinsey[6] concludes that it is not the amount of investment dollars and the consistency of allocation that determine future growth but the manner in which these dollars are allocated, that is, whether the allocation is based on constant reassessment of performance and readjustment based on market opportunities. It contends that there is a tendency among most companies to take an incremental approach to allocating resources and following the same broad investment pattern. However, higher shareholder returns are achieved by those who constantly reevaluate the situation and allocate resources based on market opportunities. This raises another differentiation for software companies when it comes to R&D. Manufacturing industries are more amenable to and more likely to adopt incremental investment patterns,[7] but for software companies this strategy is not a good option, as Myspace, Yahoo, and even Microsoft (mobile OS) are finding out. Furthermore, they (manufacturing industries) tend to manage R&D projects from a project management perspective rather than from an innovation management point of view. For example, Engwall and Jerbrant talk about a "mature and comprehensive system for *project management*" with regard to product development in a traditional company versus "immature, crude, and unsophisticated" procedures in the R&D department of a technology company.[8] They also distinguish between the former having to deal with technical uncertainties compared to market uncertainties for the latter. Generally, cutting-edge innovation has to deal with both technical and market uncertainties, the Tesla electric car being one example.

Defining Innovation

There have been attempts at measuring R&D effectiveness by measuring, for example, the number of new products launched or the sales generated by new products as a percentage of total sales and so on. For example, Werner and Souder[9] give the following examples of quantitative-objective metrics frequently reported in academic literature on R&D:

- R&D Effectiveness Index = Revenue generated from products introduced in a specified prior period (e.g., three years) as a fraction of total R&D spend
- R&D Innovation Index = Revenue generated from products introduced in a specified prior period (e.g., three years) as a fraction of total revenues
- R&D Quality Index = Ratio of the number of products and services introduced in a specified prior period (e.g., three years) and the number of customer needs
- Number of patents or intellectual property that generate value for the company as a percentage of total patents or intellectual property

Others have tweaked the aforementioned to arrive at their own metrics.[10]

It will be immediately evident that there are problems when such metrics are blindly applied to software companies. Traditionally, revenue is generated through sale of products or services, but for most online companies the product/service is provided free. Revenue is generated indirectly and therefore it is more a function of monetization strategy than of R&D effort. This renders the effectiveness and innovation indices unsuitable as measures of R&D efficacy. Even the quality index is deficient because by definition companies like Google and Samsung may score well but Apple may not, even though Apple is known for efficient utilization of its R&D dollars.

These methods do not have answers on (a) how to assign value to different R&D proposals with a view to filtering out the best for allocating scarce resources ("value" being measured in terms of which projects offer the most returns); and (b) how to measure "innovation" so that companies can initiate policies and processes for maximizing it. Both these questions are important for the software industry. One of the underlying reasons for this difficulty in achieving lasting R&D productivity improvements is that, unlike other functions of the organizations, there is a lack of repetitive tasks in R&D measuring. Furthermore, R&D departments tend to have very poor relationships with other departments such as Finance. For example, Szakonyi, citing the case of a health care products company, observed that due to limited interactions with Finance and Accounting department members of the R&D department have very little knowledge about the financial affairs of their company. The reverse is also true because the finance department too has little understanding about what is going on at R&D. [11]

Finally, there are management biases toward resource allocation, project prioritization, and inter-project rivalries that muddle the situation. These issues not only complicate the measurement of R&D value but also hamper generation of lasting R&D-productivity improvements.

Even lasting R&D-productivity improvements are not the end of the narrative because they presuppose an element of incremental change rather than disruptive innovation, which seems to be the norm for the software industry. Therefore, before we proceed further let us begin by defining "innovation."

Definition: Innovation Is Change That Produces Customer Value

The inclusion of the term "*customer*" as differentiator of value is important in our context because eventually value has to be seen from the point of view of the customer, otherwise the financial value-add to the company would be limited. There are other versions of the definition. For example, according to Maxwell, "differentiated value ... is innovation,"[12] while Nagji and Tuff [13] prefer to use the term "novel creation" instead of change and omit the word "customer." They state that this change or novel creation can be classified into three different categories according to the "Innovation Ambition" of the company:

- Core—Building on existing products for existing customers
- Adjacent—Expanding scope of existing business into "new to the company" areas
- Transformational—Developing breakthroughs targeting markets that don't yet exist[14]

In the past it may have been possible to survive by sticking to core innovation initiatives, especially for consumer product companies, and occasionally venturing into adjacent territory. According to Nagji and Tuff, "firms that excel at total innovation management simultaneously invest at three levels of ambition, carefully managing the balance among them."[15] Their ideal recipe varies with industry, from 70:20:10 for consumer goods companies to 45:40:15 for technology companies (Nagji and Tuff 2012). For software companies, the pace of change is so disruptive that a different split may apply. For example, Google follows a 70:20:10 split where:

- 70 percent of their projects are dedicated to their core business
- 20 percent of their projects are related to their core business
- 10 percent of their projects are unrelated to their core business.[16]

The distribution may require to be tweaked depending on the type of software industry—online players operate in a more disruptive environment so that there can be more emphasis on the transformational category, whereas outsourcing companies, which operate in a comparatively less disruptive environment, could focus more on core and adjacent categories. Transformational goals can be achieved through acquisitions, for example, Facebook's acquisition of WhatsApp and Microsoft's acquisition of Skype, or organic such as Google and Apple (although they are also prolific acquirers).

Elements of Innovation

Once the "Innovation Ambition" is in place the next step is managing innovation. A Booz & Company study[17] reveals that it is not the innovation strategy per se but how it is managed that is key to better financial performance:

> *The success of each of the strategies depends on how closely companies, in pursuing innovation, align their innovation strategy with their business strategy and how much effort they devote to directly understanding the needs of end-users … Companies that can craft a tightly focused set of innovation capabilities in line with their particular innovation strategy—and then align them with other enterprise-wide capabilities and their overall business strategy—will get a better return on the resources they invest in innovation.*[18]

This underscores the role of the chief executive officer (CEO) not only in setting the innovation strategy but also in ensuring that the requisite innovation capabilities are in place. Once this is done the successful innovation management depends on the following three factors:

1. Breeding and fostering agents of innovation in a company
2. Managing and aligning their direction so as to the serve strategic goals of the company
3. Identifying and filtering efficiently and effectively so that good ideas are not lost and bad ones not pursued

Breeding and fostering agents of innovation in a company. Managing innovation strategically is not a top-down exercise. It requires building an organization structure that fosters innovation at every layer, otherwise good ideas would die before they are able to reach maturity. For example, Google allows its employees to spend a portion of their official time every week to their pet ideas. This policy led to the development of such well-known products as Google News, Gmail, and AdSense. Some companies like Cisco resort to "crowdsourcing" of ideas, that is, encouraging their employees to come up with new ideas. On the other hand, Microsoft, which had a more traditional structure, had to embark upon a major cultural shift, spearheaded by Bill Gates himself, when they made the transformational decision to move from stand-alone to Internet-compatible products.

Managing and aligning direction of agents of innovation. Channeling ideas in the right direction is also very important. Innovation must be aligned with the company's overall growth strategy as well as with the skills and resources available. Pursuing disparate ideas would spread the resources thin, diffuse management focus, and the company may not possess the proper skill sets required to develop some of the ideas. Senior management has a crucial role in ensuring that the company's culture and skill sets are in line with the demands of technological change. Booz & Company[19] has listed three types of company cultures:

1. Need Seekers: keenly study existing and potential customers to develop and market new products and services before anyone else
2. Market Readers: diligently track their customers and competitors and achieve value creation through incremental change and by capitalizing on proven market trends
3. Technology Drivers: develop new offerings by leveraging their technological capabilities, often addressing unarticulated customer needs through breakthrough innovation

For software companies it is probably necessary to follow a combination of all three—a good example being how Facebook has morphed from a simple social networking company to a comprehensive offering of networking, news, chatting, and so on, through a collection of 10 companies that includes WhatsApp and Instagram. Google is another example of this combined strategy.

Identifying and filtering efficiently and effectively. The R&D value chain consists of four main stages—ideation, selection, development, and commercialization. It is important that, as they move through this funnel, good ideas are not lost and bad ones not pursued. This not only requires keeping abreast of trends in technology but also awareness of existing and potential customer needs. The role of top management in this is vital as evidenced by Apple's Jobs, Facebook's Zuckerberg, Amazon's Bezos, and PayPal's cofounder Musk.

In short, successful innovation strategies depend on the ability of a company to insightfully comprehend technological trends so as to come up with solutions not only for customers' unmet needs but also those that they may not even be aware of. This requires an intimate knowledge of the trends in customer universe and the organizational agility to extract and exploit any available opportunity therefrom. This has led to the race to acquire massive amounts of data about users and the rise of data analytics.

Measuring Innovation

Given all the aforementioned, how does one measure innovation? It is clear that innovation is inextricably linked to a steady stream of new ideas. A company's success at innovation is determined by how efficaciously it is able to identify potential winners and nurture them into customer offerings. To get a quantitative measure of idea generation we can consider "innovation success rate," which is defined as:

$$\text{Innovation success percentage (ISP)} = \frac{\text{Number of successful ideas}}{\text{Total number of ideas generated}} \times 100$$

However, this measure is not as simplistic as it sounds because of a number of subjective parameters that enter into the equation. For example, the success of an idea depends not only on its inherent properties (novelty, utility, need satisfaction, appeal, etc.) but more importantly on the diligence with which it is implemented. As any venture capitalist will confirm, success lies as much in backing winners as in working with dedicated and resourceful entrepreneurs who can overcome obstacles and make their business ideas a success. Another issue is how aggressively the idea is pursued; in other words, one has to really "go for it" otherwise it is bound to flounder and possibly fail. Finally, there is the issue of what is a good ISP figure that a company should aim for—5 percent,

10 percent, or more. Here the venture capital industry provides a good pointer. According to one venture capitalist loss ratios have shown that about 30 percent of ideas pursued give more than 2× return while another states that 15 percent of ideas give more than 3× returns and 7 percent give more than 5× returns.[20] For the innovative company, an ISP figure between 5 and 10 percent could be an aspirational figure depending on its innovation profile.

However, the aforementioned measure does not involve a financial yardstick, which is always preferable from the strategic managerial accounting (SMA) perspective. We can measure the financial commitment to the company's innovation efforts by another parameter—innovation focus (IF), which is defined as follows:

$$IF = \frac{\text{Funds invested in ideas explored}}{\text{Total number of successful ideas}}$$

The metric gives the investment per successful idea and is a useful figure to track year-on-year. If the investment in a particular project is higher than the company IF then one needs to carefully monitor the contribution of that project. This metric is useful as it sensitizes the company as to whether it is running after too many ideas or is investing too little for idea generation.

This brings us to the third metric—innovation productivity (IP), which is defined as:

$$IP = \frac{\text{Revenue contributed by successful ideas}}{\text{Number of successful ideas}}$$

This metric not only measures the value of winners backed by the company but also the success of efforts to monetize those ideas. Finally, there is a purely financial metric that measures innovation in terms of money—innovation efficiency (IE), which is defined as:

$$IE = \frac{\text{Revenue contributed by successful ideas}}{\text{Total amount spent in generating new ideas}}$$

This is the same as the R&D Effectiveness Index mentioned earlier in the context of more conventional industries.

Other Considerations

While the aforementioned measures for innovation are a useful tool for monitoring the innovativeness of a company, the fact remains that sustained innovative advantage requires a combination of the right corporate culture, vision, and policy-making process. For example, Google has identified the following strategic principles that it attributes to its success at being an innovative organization.[21]

1. *Be ready to push the envelope.* Google terms this as "Think 10×," that is, true innovation happens when you try to improve something by 10 times rather than by 10 percent. According to the company, "A 10 × goal forces you to rethink an idea entirely. It pushes you beyond existing models and forces you to totally reimagine how to approach it."

2. *Listen carefully to user feedback.* In the "olden days" when stand-alone computing was the order of the day, announcing a product before it was ready for launch was considered borderline ethical because it unfairly preempted competition. Now it the era of "beta launches," where trial versions of often half-baked products are not only announced but also launched. During the beta phase, the company carefully monitors customer feedback and constantly upgrades and improves according to user preferences. This cuts short "time-to-market" and at the same time lets the user decide on the finer aspects of product features rather than a marketer or an R&D person. The Android Operating System is a prime example of this approach. According to Google, "The beauty of this approach is that you get real-world user feedback and never get too far from what the market wants."

3. *Hire the right people.* Traditional methods of hiring may not be entirely applicable for innovative companies. (Facebook's "hackathon" competition is an example of how programming talent can be identified.) Google hires for "capability and learning ability" before it hires for expertise.

4. *Look for ideas everywhere.* Good ideas are not the monopoly of R&D departments. Not only the entire workforce but even the user base can be tapped for new ideas. Just like Cisco mentioned earlier, Google "crowdsources" ideas from its employees.

5. *Go by data not opinions.* Data Analytics has become an integral part of corporate decision-making, with huge amounts of data ("Big Data") being generated online. Its accuracy and scope are far superior to opinions or even traditional market research.

6. *Focus on users not competition.* Google believes that "[i]f you can build a robust and loyal base of people who love what you do, you'll have something rare and valuable." Apple's corporate strategy is also based on this principle and has been just as successful.

Any company that wants to continue to innovate the first step, according to Google, has to "get the culture right." This requires three attributes, namely:

- Agility—the nimbleness to seize opportunities as they emerge
- Adaptability—ability to adjust to and accommodate a changing environment in a way that sustained innovation comes through planning and not providence, and
- Resilience—ability to bounce back from adversity

In some ways these three are interconnected—resilience and agility contribute toward adaptability. In turn, these may be inversely correlated with efficiency. High efficiency demands minimum resource utilization for maximum results, whereas reliance and adaptability require certain redundancies and reserves to be maintained for dealing with difficult times. Furthermore, efficiency seeks to eliminate "waste," that is, those resources that are deemed not currently required for producing results, which limits the adaptability of organizations. Indeed quite a few companies that were held up as shining examples of superlative efficiency turned out to be too inflexible and failed when faced with significant change in their operational environment. Therefore, while there is a need for trade-off between efficiency and adaptability, there is no optimal prescription for it and hence in a fast-changing environment, leadership will always be an art. However,

the best leaders have been the ones who recognized the inescapable limitations of forecasting and planning in a complex adaptive system, and consequently sought to maximize the resiliency and adaptability of their organizations, subject to achieving the levels of effectiveness and efficiency needed to escape selection—that is, to survive over a given period.[22]

Given all these, from our perspective, we can formulate metrics for the three attributes by defining the following indices.

Agility Index (AgI)—number of ideas implemented per unit time (quarter, semiannual, or annual). This index encompasses a number of parameters: the "time-to-market" capability, the fertility of new ideas, closeness to trending customer needs, and so on. An increasing trend of this metric is desirable.

$$AgI = \frac{\text{Number of ideas implemented}}{\text{Time}\left(\text{quarter, half year or one year}\right)}$$

Adaptability Index (AdI)—number of pursued ideas outside the company's core strategic interests divided by the total number of ideas pursued. One can see the importance of this metric in some of the projects being pursued by software and information technology (IT) companies such as the autonomous vehicles, space exploration, and use of drones for diverse activities such as merchandise delivery and global Internet service. The company leadership has to decide the optimal ratio that balances the need to focus on core interests with the need to be prepared for significant change in environment.

$$AdI = \frac{\text{Number of pursued ideas outside company's core}}{\text{Total number of ideas pursued}}$$

Resilience—number of pursued ideas that failed divided by the number of ideas pursued. A low or declining figure indicates that the company is resilient and has enough ammunition to recover from a failure and move to other ideas.

$$\text{Resilience Index}\left(\text{ReI}\right) = \frac{\text{Number of pursued ideas}}{\text{Total number of ideas pursued}}$$

An important indicator of resilience is the philosophy of "embracing failure" rather than seeing it as a stigma. According to Google, not failing often indicates that one is not trying hard enough, and if a product fails to reach its potential it is withdrawn but the company extracts all the useful features from it.[23]

Conclusion

In conclusion, *Innovation* remains a subjective measure and a challenge for a company's leadership. Therefore, it is as much an indicator of an organization's strategic capability as it is a reflection of the competency of its leadership. While this is key for any commercial enterprise, it is especially vital for the software industry. Even though this chapter attempts to provide some metrics for this elusive parameter, there is no universal prescription and therefore leadership in a fast-changing environment will continue to be an art. From the SMA perspective, there is also the fact that the information required for the metrics discussed earlier is always confidential, and therefore one cannot benchmark one's standing with competitors, which puts an additional burden on the company leadership in tracking their performance.

CHAPTER 7

Measuring Company Performance and Survivability in the Online Environment

What's measured improves.

—Peter F. Drucker

The last few years have seen a phenomenal rise in the number of Internet companies prompting the *Economist*, in 2011, to talk about "another digital gold rush" as "Internet companies are booming again."[1] This has been accompanied by (and is probably a result of) the feverish growth and adoption of a host of disruptive technologies like cloud computing, mobile computing, mobile banking and payment systems, e-commerce, and business process management (BPM) that are transforming the way we interact and do business. From e-commerce giants such as Amazon and Alibaba, to platform aggregators such as Uber and Kickstarter; from MMOGs[2] by Sony and Microsoft, to social media by Facebook and Twitter; and of course the myriads of apps, online companies have completely rewritten the rules of doing business and necessitated new metrics in measuring and monitoring company performance. This article examines some of the metrics of this new economy where the most prevalent business model is the Software as a Service (SaaS) model. While the SaaS model forms the basis for the following discussion, the basic tenets can be extended for other models of service also.

Basic Concepts

The customer pays what he or she perceives as the value of the product/service; therefore, a company is viable only if its costs of offering the product or service are less than the perceived value. The difference between the two is the value created by the company. Part of this value is passed on to the customer (consumer surplus) while the rest is retained by the company (captured value). Figure 7.1 depicts this relationship using arbitrary percentages. The challenge for companies is not only to maximize value creation but also to strike a balance between consumer surplus, which attracts customers (i.e., increases revenue), and value capture, which increases profitability.

Two things are evident from the previous discussion—that perceived value should be greater than the cost for the company to make profits; and profits can be maximized by either increasing customer perceived value (i.e., making the pie bigger) or by reducing costs (better efficiency). Companies strive to maximize value through value innovation, either by introducing new and innovative products and services or by tweaking existing ones. However, the story does not end with value innovation, as many start-ups have realized to their disadvantage. The value has to be captured in order to generate profits. In the first Internet boom at the turn of the century there was an explosion of value innovation, attracting hordes of new users. New companies were able to quickly build large user

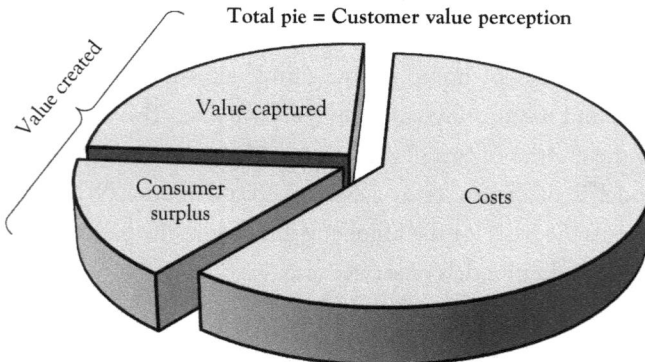

Figure 7.1 The value pie

bases with their new and innovative ideas, leading to a rush of investments at unrealistic valuations. What was missing however, was value capture, which led to the bust that followed, but not before burning through millions of dollars of investments. Therefore, while companies were able to generate unbelievable fan following through customer perceived value (CPV), they did not have a clear idea as to how to capture that value till Google happened.

The other outcome of the technology and environment of the Internet is the proliferation of a very wide variety of multisided platforms. A platform is a product, service, or system providing a technological environment that allows different types of users and complementary business partners to interact and benefit from the platform's underlying functionality. Therefore, **price setting** is a more complex and delicate balancing act. A multisided platform has multiple types of clients (sides) and therefore has the choice of pricing each of the sides differently. For online companies, often one of the sides is free and revenue is generated through the remaining sides (e.g., Facebook is free to its users, but generates revenue from advertisers and direct marketers). This captures some of the value and avoids the one-way street that led to the downfall of the early Internet companies. However, this arrangement spawns fresh complexity in the competitive advantage scenario of which the most important the is "winner takes all" aspect. For example, it is difficult for competitors to coexist with Facebook or Twitter in the exact same social media space. Therefore, the dynamics of acquisition, retention, and management of customers changes significantly. There is a mad rush for acquiring the maximum number of users as quickly as possible without regard to value capture.

Another aspect of this dynamic is **timing**. In the traditional business, the company realizes the value of goods at the time of purchase, that is, the timing is immediate. Note that deferred payments involve a different loop—financing—and hence do not affect the basic timing of the transaction. For online companies that follow the SaaS model, the timing is generally spread over an indefinite period in the form of a periodic (monthly) subscription. So the company first incurs an expense in acquiring a customer and then recovers that investment, hopefully, over the period it can retain the customer—the customer lifetime (CL). The revenue stream exists only as long as the customer is happy with the service, that is, finds value, and therefore sticks around. On the other hand, if the customer does not find value he or she would drop the service and leave. Therefore, the company has to achieve two sales for each customer: one for acquiring the customer and the other to retain him or her as long as possible. This is fundamentally different from other software business models such as product selling and outsourcing.

Metrics for Company Performance

There is another important departure from the traditional scenario where the focus is on customer acquisition alone. Here there are two more dimensions—customer retention and customer monetization, and, as a consequence, some important metrics emerge.

1. Customer acquisition cost (CAC)
2. Customer churn rate
3. Customer Lifetime (CL)
4. Average recurring revenue per account (ARRA)
5. Customer lifetime value (CLV)

Let us examine these in greater detail.

Customer Acquisition Cost

We have seen that the "winner takes all" aspect of SaaS business results in a great urgency for acquiring as many customers as possible in the shortest possible time. This makes it important to monitor and control the cost the company incurs in acquiring customers. The CAC is the cost a company incurs in acquiring one customer. If the CAC is $400 and the customer pays a monthly subscription of $39.95 for eight months and then leaves, the cash flow graph of the company for the lifetime of the customer would look like the one shown in Figure 7.2 (assuming that the first subscription is paid in the month following the acquisition).

Note that for this single customer case, the total revenue generated from the customer (8 × 39.95 = $319.60) is less than the CAC of $400.

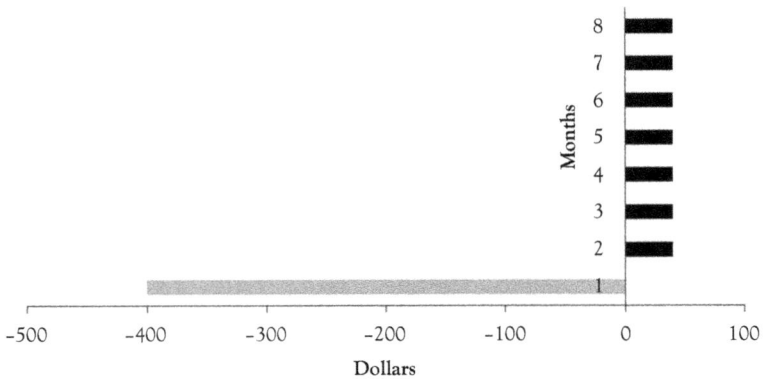

Figure 7.2 *Single customer cash flow*

This underscores the importance of retaining the customer for as long as possible. In real life, the company deals with multiple customers simultaneously; so the general formula for CAC is:

$$CAC = \frac{\left(\text{Total marketing and selling expenses for the period}\right)}{\left(\text{No. of customers added during the period}\right)}$$

Customer Churn Rate

As customers come and leave on a regular basis, a measure is required for this change. Customer churn rate is the percentage of customers who drop out every month. Note that since churn is measured as a percentage, it varies as an exponential function similar to the way depreciation behaves under the written down value (WDV) method. If a company has a churn of 10 percent, that is, it loses a net of 10 percent of its *existing* customers every month, then churn is a nonlinear function as can be seen by the shape of the graph in Figure 7.3.

Customer Lifetime

As we have seen, in the SaaS model, revenue generated from a customer is spread over a period; it is important to track the period for which the company is able to retain a customer, that is, the lifetime of the customer. In simple terms, this is the measure of the time a customer remains with

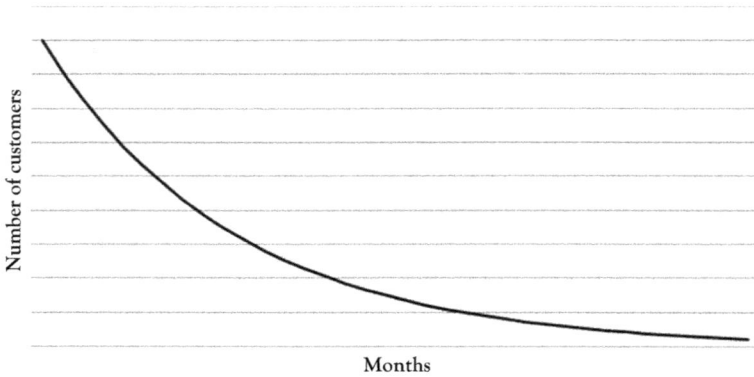

Figure 7.3 Decay due to customer churn

the company. However, as customers leave and new ones come on board continuously, CL is defined as the inverse of churn, that is,

$$CL = \frac{1}{\left(\text{customers churn rate}\right)}$$

Average Recurring Revenue per Account

The revenue per user is the monthly subscription paid by the customer. This is called the monthly recurring revenue of MRR. As there are multiple customers who may be paying different monthly revenues (e.g., depending on the level of service used), the general metric used is the ARRA, which is defined as:

$$ARRA = \frac{\left(\text{Total MRR for the period}\right)}{\left(\text{No. of customers during the period}\right)}$$

Customer Lifetime Value

CLV is an estimate of the total revenue generated from one customer over his or her relationship with the company. The general formula for CLV is as follows:

$$CLV = ARRA \times CL$$

As the company incurs some expense in serving its existing customers, the true measure of CLV would be net receipts from the customers (ARRA − Expense or ARRA × % Gross margin). In that case the formula would be:

$$CLV = ARRA \times (\% \text{ Gross margin}) \times CL$$

$$= \frac{(ARRA \times \% \text{ Gross margin})}{(\text{Customer churn rate})}$$

Note that this formula is for a business that generates recurring monthly revenue, a common SaaS business model. Different business models have different methodology (and nomenclature) for estimating the lifetime value of a customer. Also, as we are dealing with a relatively short period here, time value of money has been ignored.

Strategic Considerations

It would be clear from the previous discussion that apart from acquiring and retaining customers it is necessary that CLV be greater than CAC to get positive net cash flow. However, the behavior of these parameters needs to be understood to avoid pitfalls in making decisions. Furthermore, as customer attrition is inevitable churn also enters the picture. As churn is a nonlinear function its combination with CAC and CLV also results in a nonlinear relationship, giving rise to some strategic challenges as the following case study shows.

Case Study.[3] *Deepak Shah, chief executive officer (CEO) of Qwik-Deal Private Limited, was feeling slightly relieved as he got down to making the company's product launch plan. After 12 months of effort by three dedicated developers, QwikDeal has developed an online time and expense management software that allows companies, groups, and even individuals, to set up an account and track their time and expense or that of their employees. Deepak had a hard time raising funds initially and the company went through a rough patch before it was able to get an initial round of funding from a well-known* *venture capital firm. Not surprisingly, their terms were tough and stipulated that one of their nominees be part of the management team and have a say in all major decisions. The software was under rigorous testing and would be ready for launch within four weeks. In all, it would cost QwikDeal $550,000 for the development, testing, and implementation of the software.*

After considerable research and talking to his friends familiar with this industry he had zeroed in on the following marketing strategy:

1. *The company would start with a massive e-mail campaign supported aggressively by online advertising through Google AdWords, Facebook pages, and viral marketing.*
2. *Deepak also had got one sales rep on board who would directly sell to targeted important customers in his spare time purely on a commission basis.*
3. *Deepak estimates that the cost of servicing customers would be about 18 percent of the monthly revenue.*
4. *Pricing of the product would be as follows:*
   (a) *Based on the budgeted marketing cost, Deepak calculated the cost of acquiring a customer to be $6500.*
   (b) *Customers would be charged per user every month. Based on the projected customer/user mix, Deepak calculated that the ARRA would be $550.*
5. *An attrition rate (churn) of 2 percent was assumed.*
6. *Deepak targeted that he would add at least 2 customers every month.*

Based on the aforementioned figures, Deepak presented his marketing plan and budget to the management team, and was relieved when the VC immediately approved it. The marketing effort went well, with two customers on board in the first month and another three in the subsequent month. However, by the third month, it was clear to Deepak that the software was catching on well and he could increase the target to as many as 12 new customers every month. Deepak's excitement knew no bounds as he aggressively went after boosting sales. The following week, the chief financial officer (CFO) of QwikDeal dropped in at Deepak's cubicle with the news that the company was rapidly burning through its cash and something needed to be done quickly before it ran out. He felt that, at this rate, *the company needed another $10 million to cover its cash needs. Although Deepak was taken aback by the huge figure, he looked at the latest customer acquisition figures and asked the CFO to rework the budget figures and send a request for fresh funds to the VC. He was sure that with this spectacular performance it could not be turned down.*

Therefore, it was a shock when reply came from the VC expressing reluctance in releasing additional funds and asking for more information. Deepak immediately confronted the VC representative in the managing committee who declined to elaborate further except to ask "If the sales are so good how come you are running short of cash?"

This is a good example of how the importance of customer retention in a SaaS environment fundamentally alters the dynamics of financial viability of a company. Let us examine the situation at QwikDeal: CLV is $22,500[4] and CAC is $6500. Therefore, at first glance, the situation seems to be good because CLV is far greater than CAC, and the team, including the VC, was happy. However, when the number of new customers increased to 12, the scenario changed considerably leading to the push back from the VC. Let us examine this in more detail.

QwikDeal's cash-flow situation is the result of two factors—monthly recurring revenue inflow and customer acquisition cost outflow. While MRR is increasing with the addition of new customers, the cost of customer acquisition (CAC) is increasing as well, resulting in a negative cash flow. However, even though MRR per customer is less that CAC, total revenue growth is a cumulative figure and hence it increases much faster than total CAC, which increases linearly. Therefore, after an initial dip, the cash flow eventually turns positive as cumulative revenue catches up with CAC, as can be seen in the cash flow graph in Figure 7.4.

From the strategic managerial accounting point of view, the cash flow trough is a significant parameter because it has a huge effect on the cash burn rate of a company, as QwikDeal learned very quickly. Should the company push ahead with its aggressive customer acquisition plan or should it pull back and go steady? To answer this let us look at what happens when the customer acquisition accelerates. Figure 7.5 gives the graph for different rates of new customer sign ups.

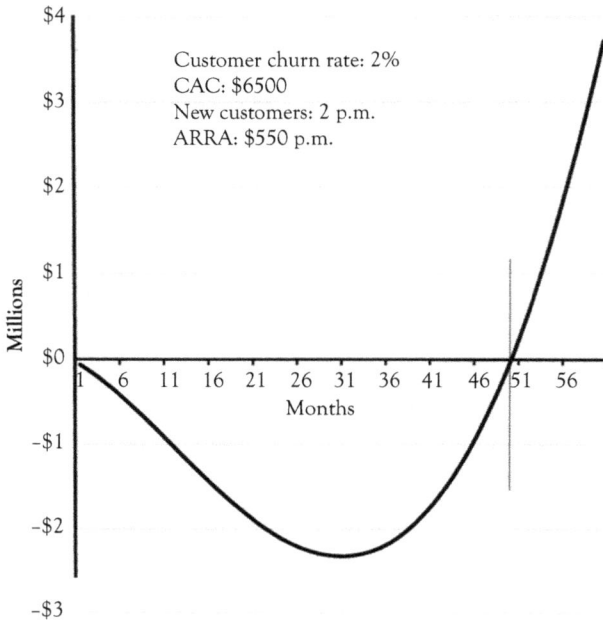

Figure 7.4 Effect of growth rate on cash flow

Two things are evident from Figure 7.5—first, the faster the growth, the deeper the trough. Second, the faster the growth the faster is the recovery from the trough. The negative peak at the 15 customer per month growth is nearly $17 million—a large sum of money for a small company like QwikDeal. However, after it turns positive the cash flow growth is much faster. Therefore, if one is willing to put up the cash, the rewards are much greater. So, should the VC go ahead and put up the extra money? The answer to that question requires study of some more relationships.

Apart from growth rate, some other factors can also affect the depth of the trough—CAC and MRR. Intuitively, it will be clear that the higher the CAC the deeper will be the trough, because more cash is burned up for acquiring customers. On the other hand, a higher MRR means a lower trough. (Why? Because the cash flow will become positive more quickly and will then offset the negative effect of the CAC.) In other words, the faster it takes to recover the CAC, the lower will be the trough. Therefore, "months to recover CAC" is another useful

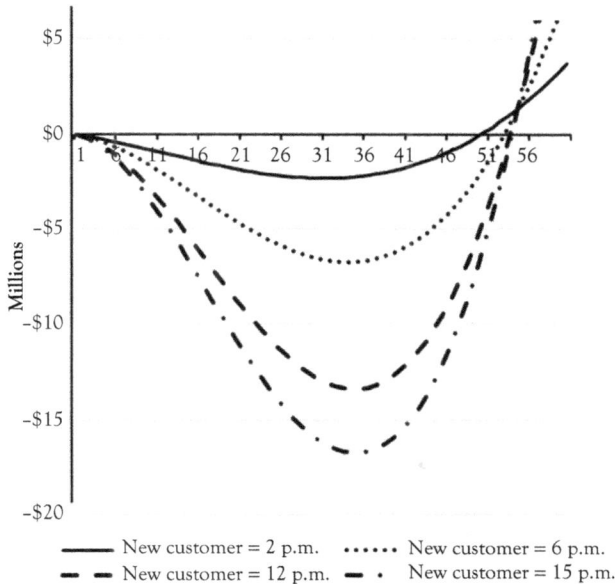

Figure 7.5 Effect of different growth rates on cash flow

performance metric. Using ARRA instead of MRR gives a more general case of this parameter. Thus,

$$\text{Months to recover CAC (MRC)} = \frac{\text{CAC}}{\text{ARRA}}$$

In the case of QwikDeal, it takes almost 50 months to recover CAC, which should normally be a cause of concern, but this will be discussed later.

Performance Ratios

The other important parameter that needs careful monitoring is churn as this is one of the most dangerous causes for company failure. As churn is generally small, it tends to be overlooked as "normal attrition" especially when the customer base is large. However, over time, its effect can be disastrous. Intuitively, churn should be less than the new customer acquisition rate because even if increasing ARRA can initially mask its effects, eventually churn will take over and lead to an irreversible decline in revenue. As CLV incorporates churn, another useful parameter for monitoring the financial health of the company is the CLV-to-CAC ratio. However,

$$\frac{CLV}{CAC} = \frac{CL}{MRC}$$

Therefore, this ratio incorporates properties of churn, CL, revenue, and so on, and is therefore an important metric for SaaS companies. Figure 7.6 shows the impact of this ratio on the cumulative cash flow. If the ratio is very low, then the company may find it difficult to get into positive cash flow territory and may continue to burn cash. Generally speaking, if the ratio is between 3 and 4, then the cumulative cash flow turns positive within the CL, which indicates good financial viability. This will also be evident from closer examination of Figure 7.6. Financially strong Internet companies have a ratio well above that. It is also important to ensure that the MRC does not extend beyond a reasonable time frame, ideally less than 12 months in order to minimize risk because the Internet environment can be very fickle and difficult to predict.

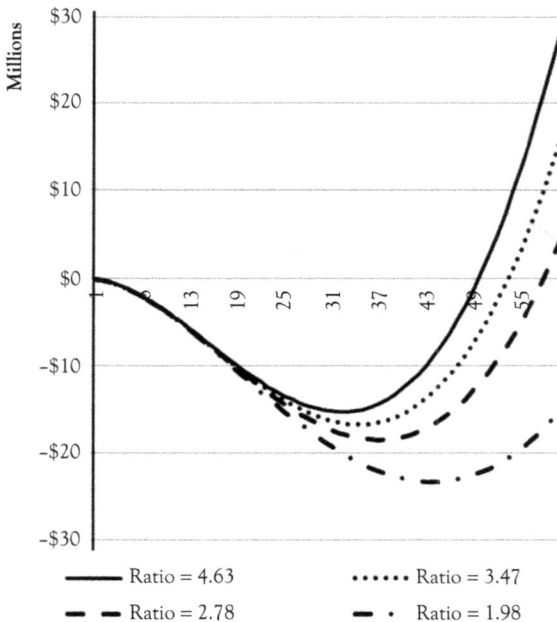

Figure 7.6 Impact of CLV–CAC ratio on cash flow

In actual practice, the financial model may be more complex than the simple case discussed, requiring mathematical tweaking of the formulas. However, rigorous mathematical treatment is beyond the scope of this book.

If we see QwikDeal's situation in light of the earlier discussion the following scenario emerges:

(a) MRC is 14.4 months, CLV-to-CAC ratio is 3.47, and two new customers are being added every month. Cumulative cash flow becomes positive in 50 months. The peak negative cash flow is $2.2 million. These parameters seem to be close to the norms mentioned earlier (MRC about 12 months and ratio greater than 3). Therefore, purely based on this analysis, the VC should support the company.

(b) When the new customer acquisition reaches 12, the company starts burning cash at a much faster rate, reaching a peak negative cash flow of 13.43 million, and the positive cash-flow point is pushed back by a month. Should the VC support the company? The answer is yes, provided they can put up the extra cash. The reason is that the rewards are much greater after the cash flow becomes positive. However, some qualitative issues arise that they need to consider as well before deciding.

Qualitative and Strategic Considerations

Qualitative

One of the common misconceptions is the idea that if CLV is greater than CAC then the project should be financially viable. While intuitively this may look like sound reasoning, the actual situation can be more complex:

(a) If the burn rate is very high, that is, the cash trough (Figure 7.4) is deeper than what the company's cash reserves can afford, the operation can collapse for want of cash even if CLV > CAC.

(b) Estimating CLV can be quite tricky—it involves estimating not only customer attrition rate and average revenue per customer but also estimating future revenue trends. A small variation in estimating churn can have a major effect on burn rate. Furthermore, there can be more than one ways of looking at averages (recurring revenue averaged over current month can be different if averaged over last three months or 12 months).

(c) CLV assumes a stable cost and revenue environment. If CLV is reckoned over an extended period, risk due to exceptional situations should not be ignored.

(d) CLV can be *historical* or *predictive* or a combination of both. Historical CLV, as the name suggests, considers past actual figures to arrive at a value, while predictive CLV looks at future projections. Both methods have their limitations.

(e) Customer acquisition costs do not necessarily remain constant. They may rise due to increased competitive activity, increase in media costs, or market saturation.

Furthermore, CLV calculations can vary considerably depending on the methodology used. Therefore, it is important to monitor variances from actual data and make suitable course corrections. Companies use sophisticated algorithms and Bayesian probabilistic techniques for estimating CLV. Companies that do not have access to these modeling techniques would do well to bear in mind the following:

(a) Every customer is different. This "customer heterogeneity" complicates not only the calculation of CLV but also the strategic approach to marketing, for example, a higher CAC is justified for more valuable customers.

(b) It is necessary to analyze individual-level buying patterns from the past to determine key customer characteristics in the data set.

(c) Identify patterns that relate to valuable customers and those that correspond to customers who are leaving for good.

(d) Classify new customers according to the aforementioned patterns to get insights into their CLV.

Strategic

As more and more software product companies are adopting the SaaS model, it is important for the managerial accountant to appreciate the fundamental characteristic of this model—every customer has a lifetime, and revenue is spread over the lifetime of the customer. This means that it is not only important to acquire a customer but also to retain him or her. Essentially, this means that the company has to accomplish two sales for each customer—one for attracting her and another for keeping her happy for as long as possible. Therefore, customer retention assumes great importance because the longer the customer continues with a company the greater she contributes to the revenue and profitability. This is fundamentally different from the situation in traditional product marketing. In this situation, the following factors are essential for the financial viability of a SaaS business:

1. Acquiring customers
2. Retaining customers
3. Monetizing customers

CAC and churn are other important metrics for managerial accountants. As companies may have different methods for reaching out to customers (AdWords, e-mail, internal sales, etc.) it is important to recognize customers according to their acquisition cost. Therefore, while spending more to acquire high-value customers companies must avoid customers whose CAC turns out to be higher than expected and exceeds the ability to monetize those customers. The other important metric—churn—also needs close monitoring and it should be the quest of companies, whether established or start-ups, to get into a negative churn[5] situation as quickly as possible. Achieving positive churn has a dramatic effect on cash flow and profitability. A related challenge is finding ways to measure customer happiness, which is so crucial to customer retention. Qualities that lead to better customer happiness include bug-free software, minimum loss of customer data, speed of response of the software, and efficient handling of customer service requests. Indicators of customer happiness are on-time payments, referral of other customers, participation in customer community activities, and so on.

Conclusion

SaaS is fast becoming the mainstream delivery model for software companies, which in turn is changing the dynamics of the way software is sold: model, the delivery mechanism, and the associated metrics. Furthermore, a major portion of the selling process is over before the customer lands at the company's website, which underscores the importance of retention. As time lines for these companies are very short due to the fast-changing environment of the Internet, the job of the strategic managerial accountant becomes not only important but also complex. An important corollary is the generation of a huge amount of data and the availability of very sophisticated analytic techniques. This data-driven environment further complicates the job of the SMA.

The challenge is to find answers to questions such as:

- Which customer acquisition method (AdWords, e-mail, etc.) is most effective and what should be the budget allocated to it
- When is it advisable to accelerate spend on customer acquisition
- What is the recipe (product, pricing, segmentation, etc.) for quickly maximizing the CLV/CAC ratio

The answers to these questions vary from application to application, and the winners are the ones who are able to figure out the right recipe. As this insight often comes from trial and error, the key is to encourage a customer feedback, monitor it very closely, and respond to their feedback very quickly. At least one company has benefited greatly by this strategy—Google.

CHAPTER 8

Employee Performance— Significance and Evaluation

You take care of the people. The people take care of the service. The service takes care of the customer. The customer takes care of the profit. The profit takes care of the re-investment. The re-investment takes care of the re-invention. The re-invention takes care of the future. (And at every step the only measure is EXCELLENCE.)

—Tom Peters 7 Steps to Sustaining Success

Case Study

Tim Allen had mixed feelings when he was asked by his company, Tele-Infora Inc. of Mountain View CA (TI), to take over as head of Personnel at their newly set up India Development Centre (IDC) at Bangalore, India. The salary raise was good and the part that would be paid in the United States would be fully saved. More importantly, he would be heading one of the key departments of IDC—the human resources (HR) department, and the international exposure would be great for his resume; hence he decided to accept.

One year ago, TI had outsourced a large part of its software development activity to India to take advantage of the big wage arbitrage and the favorable time zone. However, they were struggling with quality and productivity issues that were threatening to offset the cost saving due to outsourcing. Tim, a graduate with HR specialization from a well-known east coast business school, had joined the company four years ago. His positive and goal-oriented approach had led to a quick rise and he soon became the company's go-to person to address any difficult HR issue.

The IDC had started with great fanfare. TI had transferred a seasoned HR person from Mountain View to oversee recruitment, training, and other personnel issues. It did well initially but within six months quality started plummeting followed by missed deadlines and a drastic fall in output. More worrying was the fact that the key technical people had resigned and the attrition rate was clearly above the industry average.

Tim spent his first month in India in understanding the situation. His predecessor had apparently done a good job of implementing the best practices followed by TI in the United States—work–life balance, removing subjectivity from performance evaluation by detailed metrics that tracked everything from the number of lines coded to the number of bugs in the coding, number of hours worked, productivity in terms of code lines per hour, and so on. He had also put in place (at considerable cost to the company) a training schedule for every programming resource that did not clash with their work schedule— one hour set aside every day for training.

Tim was puzzled as to how such a thorough performance management system could fail. Discussions with team leads and programmers did not yield much. They were quiet, deferential to his authority and introverted, and the language issue added to their reticence. Meanwhile another key technical person had put in his papers and Tim decided that he would conduct the exit interview personally without anyone else from HR. The interview was revealing.

After a lot of gentle prodding by Tim, the person finally opened up. He had joined TI because he expected an excellent work culture and environment in addition to the good salary. However, he found that his work experience was not rewarding at all—on the contrary it was quite tension filled. First, the company's work–life balance policy frowned upon people working beyond office hours, while he was like most of his colleagues who preferred to work long hours at their own pace so that they could complete tasks even if their pace was slow. The training policy disturbed their work rhythm, which further affected output. This put a lot of pressure due to task deadlines, resulting in a number of good people leaving.

When the productivity suffered, the company instituted more detailed quantitative performance measures such as line of code. The programmers found it very easy to game the system—program a lot of bad code to meet the target. When an incentive for correcting number of coding errors was introduced they produced high volume of coding in quick time and the resulting error-filled code gave them the opportunity to correct more errors. This not only enabled them to score higher in the performance measure for coding output but also for number of bugs fixed. In such an environment it was very difficult for talented programmers who produced high-quality code to operate. The end result was that these good guys were filtered out and the ordinary ones who remained had even greater incentive to game the system rather that produce good code.

Introduction

Performance evaluation serves three key purposes. One, it influences people's behavior. Two, it improves organization's capabilities and competencies. Three, it helps in understanding performance consequences. While all of these are seemingly beyond the scope of management accounting and are certainly in the domain of organization behavior and HR management, they do impact costs, revenue, and profits, and hence straddle management accounting domain as well.

Results of a survey conducted in 1998[1] indicated that companies that used performance management system had larger margins, a better cash flow, higher stock exchange ratings, and higher market capitalization. The survey was revisited in 2005 and the finding was that performance management had acquired a more central role in strategic management. The survey brought out the fact that performance management is the primary means by which "a line of sight" can be created between strategic goals of the organization and individual activity and behavior.

General Principles

Any commercial activity basically involves three elements: Input → Processing → Output. We start with inputs, process them to turn them into outputs. Or, to put it differently, capital is applied to resources to generate revenue (Figure 8.1). The relative importance of each of these elements depends on the type of commercial activity. On a very general level, the processing segment becomes strategically important for capital-intensive companies such as steel plants. For manufacturing-intensive companies such as the automotive industry, both input and processing segments assume importance, while the processing and output segments are significant for innovation and research and development (R&D)-focused companies.

INPUT		PROCESSING		OUTPUT
Direct materials Direct labor Indirect costs	⇨	Funds Infrastructure	⇨	Goods Services
Resources		Capital		Revenue

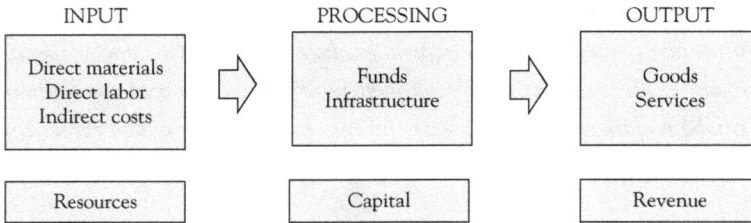

Figure 8.1 *Elements of a commercial operation*

For the software industry however, input is mainly effort (person hours) and the output is mainly a service[2] and its cost structure makes only the input and output segments important. Therefore, these should be the focus of their performance evaluation process. The strategically important goal is maximization of the monetary value of output and minimization of the cost of effort consumed in producing it. This implies that, for sustained competitive advantage, companies have to reduce cost of effort per capita (CPC) or increase revenue per capita (RPC). CPC is a function of a company's wage structure while RPC is a reflection of skills it possesses. (The implications of RPC have been discussed in more detail in Chapter 5.) Initially, Indian software development companies thrived on low CPC due to the wage arbitrage, a phenomenon termed as "body shopping." However, as competition increased, customers were willing to pay less and less for the same services, that is, RPC declined for the same level of service. This has resulted in a quest for moving up the value chain by improving the skill sets of employees.

Outsourcing Companies and the Bell Curve

As mentioned earlier for software development service (outsourcing) companies, the areas of focus are the input and output, that is, resource utilization and revenue generation. Minimization of costs at the input level means reducing the cost per hour of effort, which in turn means lower CPC. In the past when the wage arbitrage between a U.S. developer and his or her counterpart in India was large, the emphasis was on increasing personnel count with cursory attention to talent and skill. Therefore, companies were inclined to adopt the "bell curve" for eliminating the "nonperformers" who made the bottom decile of the curve.[3]

However, the bell curve performance metric suffers from serious deficiencies. First, it starts with the assumption that the skill distribution and performance output are normal (bell curve) symmetrical distribution with equal number of people on either side of the mean. However, as the lower decile of the universe is eliminated, the curve keeps getting narrow and the mean shifts toward the higher performers.[4] Normally this should be good for the company because it results in the improvement of the average performance level of the company. However, there are serious fallouts as we will see below.

It will be immediately evident that, over time, as the company sheds the bottom decile, even those who would normally be considered satisfactory performers will find themselves facing the axe. Figure 8.2 shows the changing scenario of performance distribution. As managers are forced to mark 10 percent of their team as "nonperformers," with the result that, with a narrowing gap in the levels of performance, evaluations would be made on subjective (i.e., visible) rather than actual performance. For example, work done on resolving a customer emergency (a highly visible act) could get rewarded more that work done to preempt such emergencies.[5] Furthermore, as we saw in the aforementioned case study, employees soon find ways of gaming the system and shift focus on doing what gives them greater visibility rather than what might actually be more beneficial for the company. Consequently, a high performer, demotivated by such artificial demotion, behaves like a mediocre focusing more on visible tasks thereby negatively impacting the morale and social capital of the

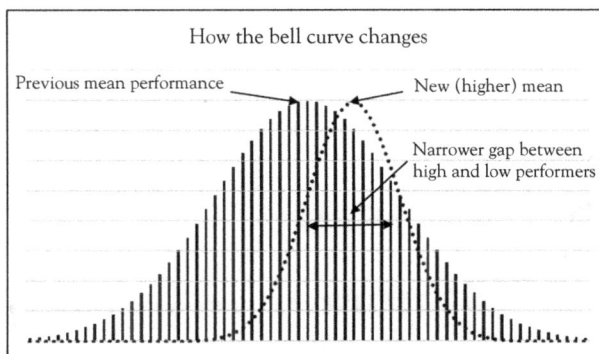

Figure 8.2 How the bell curve changes over time

company. The picture is further complicated when we take into account fresh recruitment. As the mean performance level keeps rising it becomes necessary to keep raising the quality of new recruitment. This becomes a challenge when the company has to recruit 20,000 to 30,000 people every year which was the norm for Indian software companies a decade ago when the industry was growing at 30 percent annually.

However, with rapid growth in outsourcing, adequate availability of talent in emerging markets such as India, and substantial wage arbitrage, the bell curve was a preferred method of performance evaluation for companies operating in that space. It was an effective way of improving the overall performance level of the company and moving up the value chain. However, over time, the adverse consequences of the bell curve started to kick in, forcing companies to respond. The problem lies in the fact that, as mentioned earlier, the bell curve assumes that the performance of employees is symmetrically distributed, with equal number of employees falling on either side of the mean. However, it has been suggested that the distribution is asymmetrical—there is a small number of star performers and a small segment of good performers, while the rest are average, as shown in Figure 8.3.

As a consequence, one by one, prominent companies have started abandoning the bell curve[6] and adopting more proactive measures that

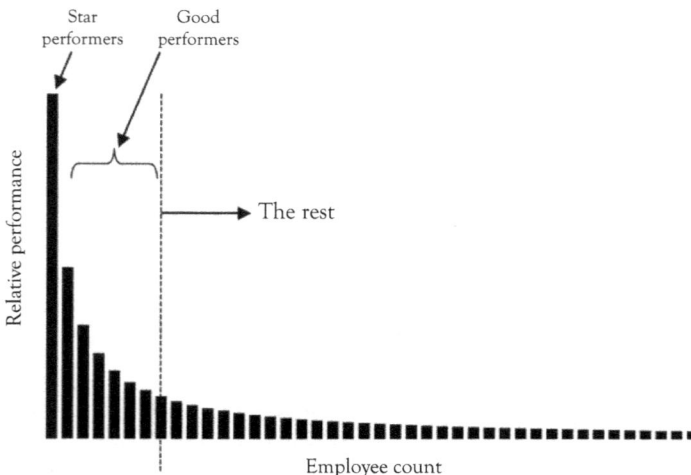

Figure 8.3 *Power Law model of performance distribution*

rate performance in absolute rather than relative terms. There is another reason for this change—the changing demographics of employees, a majority of whom (60 to 70 percent) are millennials who are demanding as well as mobile. (*You can't fire them. They will fire you.*)[7]

The Learning Curve and Its Consequences

There are other pressures influencing the way outsourcing companies are looking at employee performance. First, there is the issue of the steady gain in productivity as developers gain experience in software design and coding as well as due to streamlining of processes. This should lead to increased margins through productivity gains, but for the fact that the customers often insist on price reductions on long- and medium-term projects due to the learning curve effect. So the pressure for productivity improvement is always present, underscoring the need for close monitoring of employee performance.

Second, increasing competition puts a strain on margins, which underscores the importance of improving revenue per capita (RPC) and moving up the value chain. Companies have responded to this challenge by trying to move from *service providers* to *solution providers*. This requires a thorough understanding of both software technology and the business process and best practices of the client's industry. Furthermore, this also requires familiarity with the client's operations so as to proactively identify needs and suggest information technology (IT)-based solutions rather than wait for the client to identify an issue and then offer service or solution. For example, one of the early decisions of Vishal Sikka after he joined as the chief executive officer (CEO) of the Indian software outsourcing company Infosys was to attack declining RPC by focusing on enhancing skills by "building a team of 'super ninjas' or domain specialists across divisions to strengthen its engagement with clients."[8] They are also working on a "zero distance" initiative, whereby employees are incentivized to develop new ideas and improvements on the projects they are working on in order to create a culture of innovation that would transform their relationship with their client from a vendor to a partner.[9]

Third, rapidly changing technology requires the skill-set profile of outsourcing companies to keep evolving continuously. For example, just eight years ago, prior to the introduction of the Apple iTunes App store there was no mobile app industry, but today (2016) it is estimated to be $58 billion[10] and is expected to shoot up to $76.5 billion in 2017. This complicates the metrics for measuring employee performance because it requires accounting for a degree of obsolescence in their skill set. (Is a star performer one who is an expert in coding in some computer language or one who is proficient in acquiring the latest programming platform?)

Finally, there is the most disruptive development of all—automation of coding. With the increasing commoditization of software development services it is inevitable that the industry would move toward automation of basic coding functions. There are reports that this trend would start affecting in a big way the revenues of established players in the outsourcing industry.[11] Automation of quality assurance (QA) testing and validation (a very time- and effort-consuming exercise) is already quite pervasive with the availability of automation platforms. Overall, it has been estimated that automation and artificial intelligence (AI) have resulted in reduction of effort hours by 30 to 40 percent, and industry experts agree that this will cause a major transformation in the next five to seven years by shifting the demand from lower-level tasks such as coding, back-office maintenance, and applications testing to expertise in niche areas.[12] This means that outsourcing companies would be under increasing pressure to find engineers who can handle smart systems as opposed to recruiting in large numbers to carry out low-wage and manually repetitive operations.

Challenges and Solutions

The combination of a predominantly millennial workforce, changing customer expectations, and major shifts in technology naturally poses challenges for HR management. From the strategic perspective on one side there are the incumbents who are trying to enhance customer value by way of self-disruption through innovation and automation and niche providers focusing on business problem solving. Millennials, who comprise more than 70 percent of the workers in most software companies, are more driven and are comfortable with being measured against something they understand. They want "fast, frequent, instant and more feedback," leaving employers with little choice but to tailor their policies accordingly.[13]

The first fallout of this is the gradual discarding of the bell curve as mentioned earlier, which has already started showing results in the form of reduced attrition rate.[14] The new mantra is to engage with the employee regarding the future and not the past, which translates into holding forward-looking conversations about setting priorities, growing his or her strengths, and arriving at rewarding opportunities for career growth. The focus has shifted from performance evaluation to performance achievement and toward a holistic view that includes performance as well as potential. This means that there is more coaching and talking to employees to ensure their development rather than critiquing their performance. This approach can be facilitated by considering the concept of "Responsibility Centers" that define different sets of activities and their respective "decision rights." This is briefly dealt with in Appendix 2.

Another development is more frequent feedback on performance and commensurate action. Some companies give instant feedback to their employees on completion of a project or engagement. Some are contemplating a system of continuous feedback. For example, outsourcing major Infosys follows a system called "iCount," under which employees are rewarded based on their performance on specific short-term but important targets during the year. This approach, coupled with the performance achievement notion policy, enables the employee to work on his or her areas of development on an ongoing basis, and avoiding year-end appraisal and its related disappointments. The general refrain among HR personnel currently is *discussion* rather than *evaluation*. As one HR executive put it, the "practice of having positive, reinforcing conversations is becoming a must."[15]

The disruptive threat of digital automation is another challenge that software companies, especially outsourcing companies, are beginning to face. New recruitment has slowed down considerably as they adapt to this technology and integrate it with their business processes.

Conclusion

From the strategic managerial accounting (SMA) perspective, effective and efficient management of employee productivity and performance is a key element of competitive advantage for software companies. The changing demographics of employees and their attitudes, aspirations, and expectations have necessitated major rethinking of their evaluation methodology. The notion of employment is giving way to an "uberization" of work as millennials, who form the majority of the workforce, have a higher-risk appetite and are quite comfortable with taking up short-term projects. This makes employee retention that much harder. As a consequence, the emphasis is on a reward system based on frequent and instant feedback rather than annual appraisals. However, this change entails a major readjustment of mind-set and change in the culture and working methodology of a company.

APPENDIX 1

Case Study

Inforsystems—All Fingers of the Hand Are Not Equal!

Ramakrishnan, Vice President (Government Business) at Inforsystems, felt a sense of satisfaction as he put the finishing touch to his proposal for fresh capital investment for bidding for a new and very large government project. Ramki, as he was known to his colleagues, was sure that his proposal would be accepted by the Management. After all his division was the most important of the three divisions of Inforsystems, responsible for more than half the company's total revenue. This project would tilt the balance even further. No one would dare to question his proposal, not even the Finance department. It was too large a project to reject.

Inforsystems was a 10 year old publicly listed Software Services company that had ridden the outsourcing boom of the last decade, establishing a name for itself in the market as a reliable provider of quality software development services. The tumultuous growth in the early years had forced the company to focus more on sales rather than financial strength. None was more acutely aware of this serious problem than Padmanabhan (Paddy), the veteran CFO. He was eager to bring in fresh professional thinking in his department and had recently hired Suresh Chopra as a Manager in his department. Suresh was a young MBA with Finance Specialization, and in his previous company successfully implemented a system of evaluating projects based on a differential hurdle rate that took into account risk as well as the return. The implementation of the new system had caused a lot of uproar and unpleasantness that it eventually led to his resignation.

Inforsystems did not have a clear-cut policy regarding the rate of return to be used for evaluating different projects. At his Business School, Suresh had learned about the concept of Cost of Capital and decided to calculate the company's WACC (Weighted Average Cost of Capital). After going through all the past and present financial statements and reading the assessments of different financial analysts and investment bankers, he estimated the company's

WACC was 14%. Paddy confirmed the company was indeed using 14% as the hurdle rate for evaluating all fresh project proposals. "Here we go again" thought Suresh, thinking about his tribulations in the previous company on this very same issue.

A muted "ping" from his computer alerted Suresh that there was a new email in his inbox. He looked at the sender's name and sighed—it was Ramki's investment proposal. Suresh had already received investment proposals from the company's other two divisions—Large Accounts division and Small Accounts Division (Table A1.2). He knew about Ramki's clout with the top management, given the importance of Government business for the company. This division had shown steady growth of late, accounting for 53% of the company's business and therefore the major chunk of profits. However, since Government business consisted of large projects and took fairly long to materialize, there was considerable volatility in the business that impacted the company's overall sales and profit projections. Furthermore, payments were erratic and often delayed due to bureaucratic red tape, and the uncertainty of business meant that the company had to maintain a sizeable bench strength. Suresh wondered how this hidden cost was allocated across divisions. The other two divisions— Small Accounts and Large Accounts that equally made up the other half of the revenue were far less volatile but gave lower profits as well because most of the contracts were long term relationships with the customer.

Stock Market analysts tracking the movement of Inforsystems stock had calculated its beta (β) to be 1.18. Suresh was well aware of this situation, but he did not want to put his stamp of approval on any project without a logical calculation of the required rate of return for each division based on its volatility. He strongly believed that not doing so would result in the company making unwise capital budgeting decisions. He remembered his father's words that all fingers of the hand were not equal.

Referring to his MBA lessons, he remembered that there are two ways of calculating the risks of different divisions of a company. Rather than take the overall beta of Inforsystems and apply it to each of its divisions, one way was to study the risk of homogeneous companies in the industry in which the relevant division was operating. The industry β could then be assumed to be the β of the division and used for calculated the expected rate of return for that division. The other way was to take the WACC of the company and adjust it according to the volatility of each division. After some research Suresh decided that the *second approach would be better because proper data was not available for the first alternative. To calculate the volatility of each division, Suresh asked the accounts department to give him the sales break-up of each of the three divisions for the past 32 quarters (Table A1.1). He also gathered other relevant data which is given in Table A1.3. From these figures he calculated the variability of each division's sales and accordingly adjusted the overall hurdle rate of company to arrive at the Required Rates of Return for each division.*

After some more calculations, Suresh was ready with his recommendations—using the standard hurdle rate Ramki's proposal was by far the most favorable. However if one took into account the risk due to the volatility of government business the exact opposite was true. With a sense of uneasiness, he picked up the phone to call his boss. He knew the meeting with the division heads would not be very pleasant.

Table A1.1 Divisional breakdown of quarterly revenue

Quarter	Government	Small accounts	Large accounts	Consolidated
	Quarterly revenues—in '000s			
1	56,000	34,500	32,400	122,900
2	58,800	35,535	33,372	127,707
3	1,740	36,601	34,373	132,714
4	124,827	37,699	35,404	137,930
5	18,068	38,830	36,466	143,365
6	121,471	39,995	37,560	149,027
7	73,616	41,195	38,687	153,498
8	53,000	42,431	39,848	158,103
9	153,923	43,704	41,043	162,846
10	80,442	45,015	42,275	167,731
11	82,855	46,365	43,543	172,763
12	85,341	47,756	44,849	177,946
13	87,901	49,189	46,195	183,285
14	90,538	50,664	47,581	188,783
15	93,254	52,184	49,008	194,447
16	88,592	53,750	50,478	192,820
17	93,907	55,362	51,992	201,262
18	97,664	57,023	53,552	208,239

(Continued)

Table A1.1 (Continued)

Quarterly Revenues—in '000s				
Quarter	Government	Small accounts	Large accounts	Consolidated
19	101,570	58,734	55,159	215,463
20	105,633	60,496	56,814	222,942
21	69,858	62,311	58,518	230,687
22	114,253	64,180	60,274	238,706
23	158,822	66,106	62,082	247,010
24	123,576	68,089	63,944	255,608
25	129,754	70,131	66,502	266,388
26	86,242	72,235	68,497	276,974
27	93,054	74,402	70,552	288,008
28	200,206	76,634	73,374	300,215
29	157,717	78,934	75,575	312,226
30	215,603	81,302	77,843	324,747
31	173,883	83,741	80,178	337,801
32	188,000	86,000	82,500	356,500
	53%	24%	23%	100%

Table A1.2 Projected costs, lives, and cash inflows of divisional proposals

Division	Cost	Life	Annual net cash flow
Government	22,000	5	8,100
Small accounts	26,000	6	7,900
Large accounts	30,000	7	8,000

Table A1.3 Company data

General data	
Corporate tax rate	35%
Yield on outstanding bonds	15%
Yield on treasury bills	4%
Market risk premium (R_f)	10%
Equity	70%
Debt	30%
Beta for inforsys	1.18

Questions

1. *Using the data given in Table A1.3 explain how Suresh arrived at the figure of 14% as the company's overall hurdle rate. (For Cost of Equity use the Capital Asset Pricing Model formula)*
2. *Using the data given in Table A1.1 calculate the variability of each division's sales and compare it with the company's overall variability. Which one is the riskiest and why?*
3. *Using Suresh's methodology calculate the hurdle rate of each division.*
4. *Using the divisional hurdle rate and the data given in Table A1.2 calculate the NPV of each of the project proposals. What are your recommendations to the company's top management?*
5. *What do you think of Suresh's methodology? Can it be applied blindly or does it require some subjective managerial inputs as well.*

Suggested Discussion

The Cost of Equity can be estimated by a number different pricing models, but the simplest and most widely used is the one given by the Capital Asset Pricing Model (CAPM). According to this model

> *Cost of equity = Risk free rate of return + Premium expected for risk.*
> *Cost of equity = Risk free rate of return + Beta × (market rate of return − risk free rate of return))*
> *= Risk free rate of return + Beta × (market premium)*

The Market Premium is the premium expected for the risk associated with the stock. Risk Free Rate is generally taken to be the rate (or yield) offered by treasury bonds because they are considered risk-free.

Using this formula:
> *Cost of equity = 4% + 1.18 × 10% = 15.80%*

From Table A1.3 the Cost of debt is 15% (yield on bonds). However since this cost is tax-deductible its impact is reduced by the tax payable, i.e.

> *Cost of debt = 15% × (1 − 0.35) = 15% × 0.65 = 9.75%*

Since equity and debt are in the ratio of 70:30 the cost of capital is weighted average of these two costs, i.e.

$$Cost\ of\ capital = 15.8 \times 0.7 + 9.75 \times 0.3 = 13.985\ or\ 14\%$$

The company's hurdle rate, which is generally equal to the cost of capital, is therefore 14%.

Using Suresh's methodology the Government business is 1.68 times more variable that the Small Accounts business at shown in Table A1.4. This means that the Government business is the riskiest. Accordingly Suresh reckoned that this should be reflected in the hurdle rates for different divisions. Using the degree of variability as a measure of risk he calculated the hurdle rates of the different divisions (Table A1.4). Using these rates he also calculated the NPV of the different alternatives which revealed that the government alternative had the least NPV and hence was least preferable (Table A1.4). The calculation of NPV using the company's uniform hurdle rate and Suresh's differential hurdle rate is given in Table A1.5.

Table A1.4 Risk and other calculations

	Government	Small accounts	Large accounts
Std. deviation	47908	15319	14841
Average	105628	56597	53451
Coeff. of variation	0.45	0.27	0.28
Deg. of variability	1.68	1.00	1.03
Company cost of equity	15.80%		
Company cost of debt	9.75%		
Company WACC	13.985%		
Division hurdle rate	23.43%	13.99%	14.35%
Present value	22,502	30,733	33,947
Investment	−22000	−26000	−30000
Net present value	502	4,733	3,947

Table A1.5 Net Present Value Calculations

As per suresh's calculations	NPV	PV	Investment	Yearly cash flow						
Government	502	22,502	–22000	8100	8100	8100	8100	8100	8100	
Small accounts	4,733	30,733	–26000	7900	7900	7900	7900	7900	7900	
Large accounts	3,947	33,947	–30000	8000	8000	8000	8000	8000	8000	8000
As per Inforsystems norms										
Government	5,818	27,818	–22000	8100	8100	8100	8100	8100		
Small accounts	4,733	30,733	–26000	7900	7900	7900	7900	7900	7900	
Large accounts	4,322	34,322	–30000	8000	8000	8000	8000	8000	8000	8000

The key takeaway from Suresh's methodology is that the application of a uniform hurdle rate for businesses with different risk profiles can lead to situations that are skewed toward certain divisions at the expense of others. However it is important that these figures are used more as a pointer rather than an accurate quantitative analysis and managerial discretion is applied to arrive at differential hurdle rates after taking into account various strategic, qualitative and situational factors. Elaboration of these factors is left to the reader.

APPENDIX 2

Responsibility Centers

Any commercial activity basically involves three elements: Input →
Processing → Output. We start with inputs, process them to turn them
into outputs. Or, to put it differently, capital is applied to resources to
generate revenue (Figure A2.1). The relative importance of each of these
elements depends on the type of commercial activity. On a very general
level, the processing segment becomes strategically important for capital-intensive companies such as steel plants. For manufacturing-intensive
companies such as the automotive industry, both input and processing
segments assume importance, while the processing and output segments
are significant for innovation and research and development (R&D)-
focused companies.

For the Software Industry, however, this structure is slightly different
as shown in Figure A2.2:

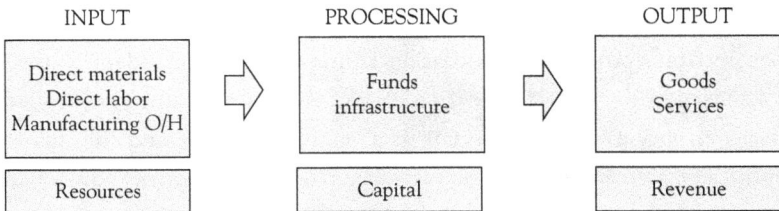

INPUT	PROCESSING	OUTPUT
Direct materials Direct labor Manufacturing O/H	Funds infrastructure	Goods Services
Resources	Capital	Revenue

Figure A2.1 Basic elements of a manufacturing enterprise

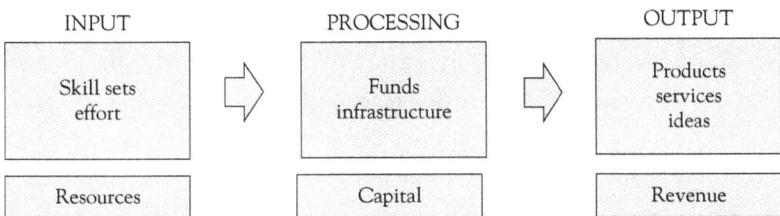

INPUT	PROCESSING	OUTPUT
Skill sets effort	Funds infrastructure	Products services ideas
Resources	Capital	Revenue

Figure A2.2 Basic elements of a Software enterprise

The cost structure of the software industry makes the input and output segments important and these should be the focus of their performance evaluation process. Furthermore, input is mainly effort (person hours) and the output is mainly a service.[1] Therefore, the strategically important goal is the maximization of the monetary value of output and minimization of cost of effort consumed in producing it. This implies that, for sustained competitive advantage, companies have to reduce cost of effort per capita (CPC) or increase revenue per capita (RPC). CPC is a function of a company's wage structure while RPC is a reflection of skills it possesses. (The implications of RPC have been discussed in more detail in Chapter 5.) Initially, Indian software development companies thrived on low CPC due to the wage arbitrage, a phenomenon termed as "body shopping." However, as competition increased, customers were willing to pay less and less for the same services, that is, RPC declined for the same level of service. This has resulted in a quest for moving up the value chain by improving the skill sets of employees.

A company's activities can also be classified into **Responsibility Centers,** which have control over different parts of the industry process. There are three main types of responsibility centers: **cost center, profit center,** and **investment center**. These centers are distinguished by the decision rights assigned to each of them. Firm owners inevitably cede some decision rights to managers, and as firms grow in size and complexity and become multiproduct, multilocation entities, firm owners identify areas for managers to exercise their decision rights. This phenomenon is called decentralization. Decentralization is a matter of degree and the nature and size of a business as well as its managerial style determines how much of it should be adopted. Decision rights assigned to a subunit are used to identify that unit as cost center, profit center, or investment center.

1. *Cost center*

   A cost center (Figure A2.3) is a unit of the company that incurs costs but does not directly earn any revenue. The manager of a cost center has control over costs but not over revenues or investments. In the process flow, a cost center only has control over inputs, but no control over the process and output:

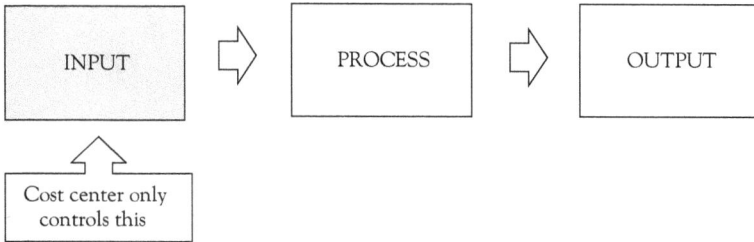

Figure A2.3 Decision rights of a cost center

Examples of a cost center are: a production unit or any of the support services like human resources (HR), finance, audit, and administration. Here *decision rights* relate to input mix, that is, people, supplies, and material. *Performance measures* for managers working in cost centers are generally based on (a) total cost incurred for a predetermined (budgeted) level of output (objective is to minimize total cost) or (b) total output for budgeted cost (objective is to maximize total output). As will be evident, quality for quantity trade-off is the major problem with these kinds of measures.

2. *Profit center*

A profit center (Figure A2.4) is a unit that not only incurs cost but also earns revenue for the company. The manager of a profit center has control over both costs and revenues but not over investments. Therefore, it (profit center) has control not only over inputs but also over the output.

For example, the sales department or a business segment has responsibility for revenue and profits; therefore, it controls both the inputs (how many people and what skill sets are to be deployed) and the output (which product/features to be produced etc.). Here *decision rights* relate not only to input mix but also to output or product/services mix and selling price, that is, managers have the freedom not only to decide on the input mix but also on areas such as output targets, product mix, and selling price. Here *performance is measured* based on accounting profit compared to budgeted profit. Problems with this measure include interdependencies of profit centers, transfer pricing, and allocation of overhead costs.

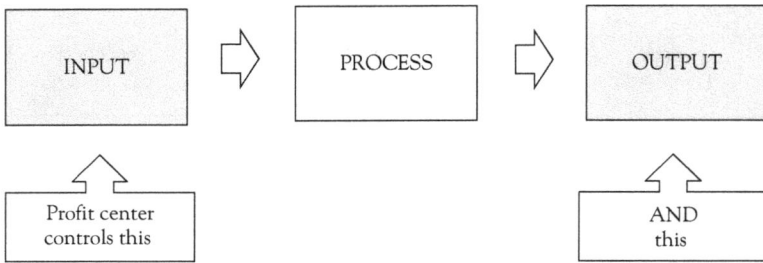

Figure A2.4 Decision rights of a profit center

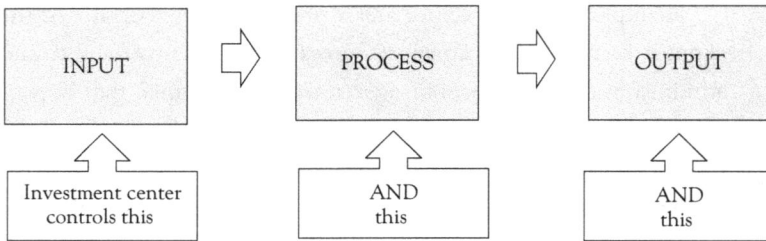

Figure A2.5 Decision rights of an investment center

3. *Investment center*

An investment center (Figure A2.5) is a unit that is responsible for committing (investing) the company's fund. Therefore, it exercises control over all parts of the process.

Therefore, its performance is measured by how efficiently it deploys the company's capital. Here managers have *decision rights* over capital investment in addition to input mix, output mix, and selling prices. Net income, return on investment, residual income, economic value added (EVA), and balanced score card are some of the *measures of performance* of an investment center. The problem with these measures (except balanced scorecard) is that they measure only financial consequences whereas nonfinancial consequences like customer satisfaction, changes in employee morale, productivity and effectiveness of business processes may be more important but completely ignored.

The decision rights criterion can be used to classify other types of responsibility centers such as revenue center (e.g., a sales and marketing unit) and discretionary expenses center (e.g., R&D division). A clear identification of every part of a business process with the relevant responsibility center leads to better alignment of company goals and employee performance evaluation system.

Multisided Platforms: Business and Revenue Models of Online Companies

In the pre-Internet world, multisided platforms have existed as business models for brick-and-mortar industries. The credit card industry is one example of this model where users (buyers), merchants (sellers), banks, and payment processors are provided with an environment where they can conduct business transactions. Even the software industry has an example of this model: the Windows platforms that connect users, hardware suppliers, and software developers. However, such examples are relatively rare. On the other hand, the technology of the Internet provides an ideal foundation for the development of multisided platforms. As a consequence multisided platforms have flourished in the online world, from aggregators like Uber and Airbnb to social media portals such as Facebook and Twitter as well as hundreds of thousands of mobile apps.

This opens up new areas and challenges for SMA such as determining monetization strategies, investment strategies, and performance metrics. Some of these issues are discussed in Chapter 7. This section provides some information on the dynamics of different types of platforms.

Platforms

A platform is a product, service, or system providing a technological environment that allows different types of users and complementary business partners to interact and benefit from the platform's underlying functionality. The business partners are called **complementors**.

As mentioned earlier, in the brick-and-mortar world companies typically engaged in producing and selling products or services. With the advent of the Internet and cloud computing, more and more companies started implementing application ideas that allow communities of participants to interact and transact business. Well-known examples are Facebook, Skype, Google Maps, and PayPal, while newer ones like Uber, which connects customers with individual taxi operators, and Airbnb, which connects accommodation seekers with people who wish to let out rooms, are mushrooming every day. To better understand this phenomenon let us examine different types of platforms in greater detail.

Let us first consider the traditional environment, that is, the brick-and-mortar world. Here physical shops provide a facility for customers to purchase goods as depicted in the Figure A3.1.

Another way at looking at the aforementioned relationship is that shops are platforms that provide a valuable input to the seller, that is, they provide a means for the seller (side A) and buyer (side B) to conduct transactions between themselves. As will be seen there is only a one-is-to-one relationship and therefore traditional shops are an example of a **one-sided platform** also called a **product platform**. Only one side (Side B in this case) is the customer who transacts with the other side, that is, Side A, with the platform only serving as a facilitator.

This relationship, though slightly modified, remains essentially similar if the platform (i.e., the shop) is used by a retailer who resells products manufactured by someone else. This relationship, depicted in Figure A3.2, constitutes a **reseller platform**.

Shopping malls provide a different type of platform as depicted in Figure A3.3.

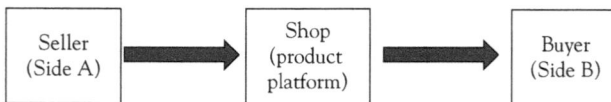

Figure A3.1 Conventional one-sided platform

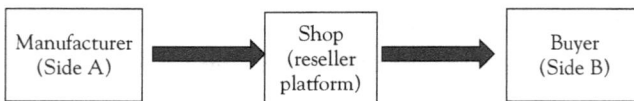

Figure A3.2 Another example of conventional platforms

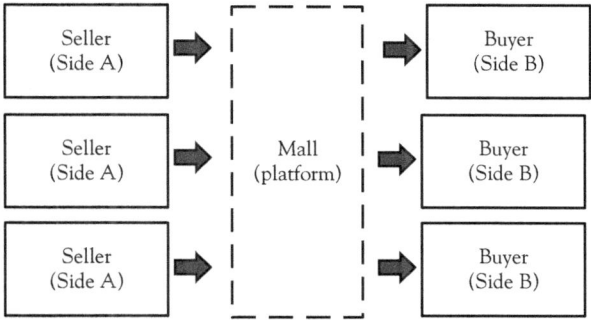

Figure A3.3 *The conventional shopping mall as a one-sided platform*

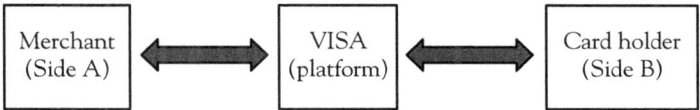

Figure A3.4 *A conventional two-sided platform*

Here only one side (Side A, the seller) is the customer of the platform (mall) because he hires retail space. The other side, that is, the buyer (Side B), transacts only with the buyer (Side A) and is not the customer of the platform. Therefore, this is also another form of a one-sided transaction because the platform makes money only from one side—side A the seller.

Now let us consider the case of a credit card company like Visa or MasterCard. The transaction flow is shown in Figure A3.4.

Here VISA provides the means for a buyer and merchant to transact by providing a platform for payment. For this both the sides pay a fee to the platform for the service that it provides.[1] This is an example of a **two-sided platform**. Sometimes the transaction cycle involves another intermediary, payment processors, who provide a specialized service. In such a case, it becomes a three-sided platform.

Similarly, there can be **multisided platforms (MSPs)** in brick-and-mortar industries that provide a means for different users to transact business that results in multiple revenue streams from multiple players. The Microsoft Windows platform is an example of a multisided platform in the physical (non-networked) world, because it provides a platform where

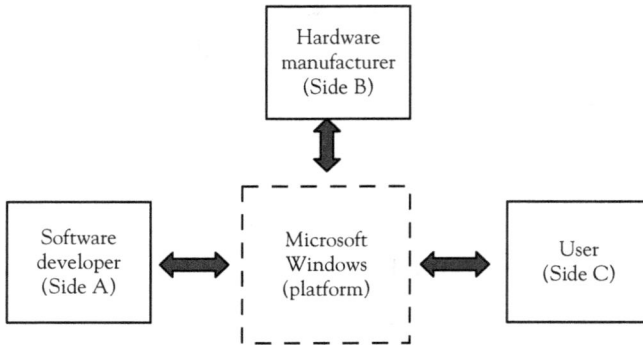

Figure A3.5 An example of a three-sided platform in the conventional computing industry

users (buyers) can transact with application developers (sellers) and hardware suppliers. All the sides generate revenue streams for the platform and the structure is shown in Figure A3.5.

Therefore, there are two essential characteristics that define a multisided platform.

1. The platform facilitates a direct interaction between two or more participants (sides)
2. Each side or group of participants is a customer of the platform in a meaningful way, irrespective of whether it is paying or non-paying.

MSPs are not very common in commercial transaction in the physical world, but in the virtual world (cyberspace) they are commonplace with varying degrees of complexity. This is because the technology of the Internet is very conducive for the design and operation of MSPs. Therefore, this latest era of the Information Age has been described as the Age of Platforms, because of the proliferation, in the virtual world, of markets defined by platform competition rather than product competition prevalent in the real world. In other words, more and more companies operating in cyberspace are offering platforms where users and providers can interface and conduct transactions directly without the need for the traditional middleman. For example, the Google Android system provides an MSP where smartphone makers, app makers, service providers (mobile and Internet), and the customers come together to create an ecosystem to transact business. With this background let us examine the different e-commerce business models that exist in cyberspace.

E-Commerce Business Models

One of the more common MSPs is the e-commerce space, which has different business models such as:

Online Shops

This business model closely resembles its counterpart in real space, that is, the traditional shop. The sellers physically stock the products they sell and use an online presence (i.e. website) to display their products, book orders, collect payments, and dispatch the goods. Most manufacturers who directly sell their products follow this model.

Online Marketplaces

An online marketplace is an e-commerce platform that enables multiple complementors to display their product, pricing, and inventory information so that customers can place their orders, with the platform operator providing the means for processing the orders. Order fulfillment is done by the respective complementor. There are two types of business models followed by online marketplaces.

Open Marketplaces

These marketplaces only connect buyers and sellers, leaving the mechanics and logistics of the transactions to the participants, that is, the buyers and sellers. A number of big online retailers follow this business model, the most prominent being eBay, the world's largest e-commerce platform, and Alibaba, the Chinese retail giant and Indian start-up OLX.com. Alibaba has created an e-commerce platform that enables small businesses and branded manufacturers alike, to connect with potential buyers. It does not participate in the sale transaction, does not sell anything directly to the customer and does not provide any warehousing facilities to its complementors.

Managed Marketplaces

These marketplaces are more akin to traditional retailing in the sense that the platform operator maintains "fulfillment centers," which aggregate orders and dispatch the goods on behalf of the complementor. Sometimes the goods may also be repacked before dispatch. Amazon, the world's largest online retailer, follows this model. It has established very large distribution centers that not only handle its own products but also act as facilitation centers for its complementors.

Other Business Models

The phenomenal success of the Uber taxi-sharing platform is an example of a new business model that is witnessing explosive growth in the virtual world. This is the **Aggregator** model of business, where the platform addresses a customer need by building a community of service providers and offers it to potential users in a convenient and efficient manner. For example, Uber provides convenient and efficient taxi service by offering a platform where car owners willing to offer a ride in their car can register and automatically connects them with customers wanting a ride. Similarly, Airbnb offers lodging services to customers from homeowners (or even small hoteliers) willing to let out their spare rooms.

The other very successful model is the **Information Sharing** portal. This includes Social Media, Microblogging (Twitter), and Image/Video sharing (Instagram, YouTube etc.). The important feature of this model is that it relies on user-generated content, that is, the portal only provides the means whereby users can upload and share their information. Other models include **Chatting and Messaging Portals,** such as WhatsApp and Skype, and **Mobile Apps**.

Loss Leaders and Revenue Drivers

As MSPs by definition have more than one possible revenue generation possibilities, the platform providers have the freedom to price their offering differently for the different sides. This assumes importance because of another characteristic of platforms, i.e. their perceived utility and

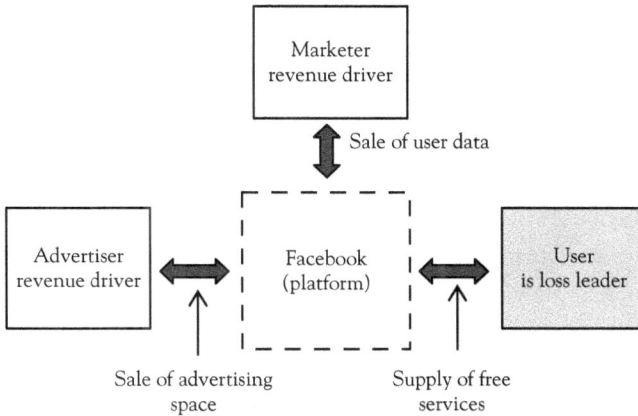

Figure A3.6 Multi-sided platforms in cyberspace

consequently their revenue-generating potential. Both grow exponentially in a virtuous cycle as more and more users sign on. This property, called network externality, demonstrates the power of networks. For platforms to succeed they need to harness the full power of network externalities, which means that they have to accumulate the maximum number of users in the shortest time. Therefore, their pricing models are such that one of the sides becomes a loss leader while the other side or sides generate revenue.

For companies like Amazon, Flipkart, and Alibaba, the user is the loss leader because they generally do not charge the user for services. The revenue-generating side is the commercial side where they make money from each transaction conducted. However, the situation becomes a bit hazy with platforms such as Facebook or Google search engine where the loss leader is the user who utilizes the service free of charge and revenue is driven either by advertising or by sale of user data to marketers. Figure A3.6 depicts the various relationships.

Revenue Models for Mobile Apps

The introduction of the iPhone by Apple in 2007 created a new industry—the smartphone—which has revolutionized mobile communications. It also led to the rapid development of mobile applications, which are now close to six million in number.[2] This segment of the software industry follows its own unique revenue models, which are briefly discussed below

In-App Advertising (free software interspersed with advertisements). In this business model, the software application is free to download but in return a lot of information is gathered about the people interacting with the app. This data is used to place targeted advertisements directed at the user. Revenue is generated from the advertisements; therefore, the goal is to get as big a user base as possible.

Freemium (free but with gated features). This is similar to the above in that a basic version of the application is free to download but premium features that add to the richness of the app are charged. A variation of this is a free version that comes with advertisements but the chargeable features are ad-free.

Paid Apps. This is the traditional model where the user pays for downloading the app. Since prices start at as low as $0.99, the idea is to attract a large number of buyers.

In-App Purchases. Here the app is free to download but revenue is generated through commissions earned through sale of physical or virtual goods. The latter happens in gaming software.

Paywalls (subscriptions). This is popular among content publishers, for example, online versions of newspapers or magazines. The user is attracted by showing a predetermined amount of content after which the users is prompted to sign in for a paid subscription.

Sponsorship (incentivized advertising). This is a new and innovative revenue model where the app developer partners with potential advertisers who display advertisements that are related in some way with the theme of the app. Therefore, the advertisement not only promotes its product but also encourages usage of the app.

Notes

Note on the IT Software Industry

1. Barber and Strack (2005).

Chapter 1

1. Orfalea and Marsh (2005).
2. Innes (1998).
3. Cooper and Kaplan (1988).
4. Bromwich (1990).
5. Lord (1996).
6. Porter (1985).
7. Houlihan (1987).
8. Riley (1987).
9. Porter (1980).
10. Shank and Govindarajan (2008).
11. Simpson and Muthler (1987).

Chapter 2

1. Figure 2.2 presents an idealized view of how fixed and variable costs behave. In reality, fixed costs may vary in steps—for example, when another office building or production plant is added. Similarly, the variable costs line may not be a straight line but a curve in reality.
2. This is an estimate based on figures from the company's 2013 Annual Report.
3. Company Annual Report.
4. Annual Report 2013 of Infosys Ltd. Personnel cost includes cost of technical subcontractors. All other costs include selling and marketing expenses (5 percent) and general and administration expenses (6 percent).
5. Magazinius et al. (2011); Lederer and Prasad (1993; 1995); Heemstra (1992); Sauer and Cuthbertson (2003); and so on.
6. Magazinius et al. (2011).
7. Moløkken and Jørgensen (2004).

Chapter 4

1. BT 500: India's Most Valuable Companies (2013).
2. Subramanian and Breslawski (1995); Magazinovic and Pernstål (2008).
3. Daniel, Hirshleifer, and Subrahmanyam (1998); Gervais and Odean (2001).
4. Einhorn and Hogarth (1978); Brehmer (1980).
5. Goel and Thakor (2008).
6. Gervais et al. (2011).
7. The coefficient of variation is the ratio of standard deviation and mean and is a good measure of dispersion.
8. Kaplan (1986).
9. Bromwich and Bhimani (1991).

Chapter 5

1. *McKinsey Quarterly* (February 2007).
2. Ameya (2014).
3. "Murthy concerned over decline in Infosys' growth". BloombergBusiness, March 13, 2014.
4. Stop Hating IBM: It's Enormously Profitable. *Blue Harbinger. Oct. 29, 2015.*
5. Company website. http://investor.accenture.com/phoenix.zhtml?c=129731 &p=quarterlyearnings
6. Source: Company Annual Reports. www.infosys.com/investors/reports-filings/annual-report/Pages/index.aspx
7. This section considers the overall financials for IBM, that is, IBM Global Technology Services, which includes its outsourcing activities, as well as IBM Global Services, the consulting arm.
8. "For All its Repurchases, IBM Isn't a Factor in Buyback ETFs". *ETFtrends. com, July 21, 2014.*
9. Better manpower utilization and higher quality of skills could be other factors for increased revenue but only up to a point.
10. The origin of the concept of this cartoon is unknown and is probably in public domain. It has existed since the 1960s and adapted by many disciplines, as has been done here.
11. Figures for FY 2015. Source: company financial statements.
12. IBM revenue has fallen from its peak in 2011 and continued to decline till 2014 because of divestment of loss-making ventures. In this discussion only the non-divested business has been taken for comparison purposes.
13. Statement by company chairman in the analysts' conference 2015.
14. "The 2015 Five Key Performance Indicators for Greater Financial Success". Service Performance Insight, LLC. Research Note. August 2015.

Chapter 6

1. "Creating a Culture of Innovation—A Google for Work perspective". (2014). *Company document.*
2. Scott (2013).
3. Maxwell (2008).
4. According to one senior executive who had the opportunity of working in both Apple and Microsoft, in product development meetings Apple engineers were able to ride roughshod over marketing and product managers, whereas at Microsoft they had to play second fiddle to the product and marketing personnel.
5. Apple watcher Neil Cybart blog (2016).
6. Hall et al. (2012).
7. Hall et al. (2012).
8. Engwall and Jerbrant (2003).
9. Werner and Souder (1997).
10. For example, McKinsey defines it as the following ratio: *R&D productivity = (Total gross contribution × Achieved product maturity)/Consumed R&D costs* However, accurately estimating factors such as "Achieved product maturity" may be tricky.
11. Szakonyi (1994).
12. Maxwell (2008).
13. Nagji and Tuff (2012).
14. Nagji and Tuff (2012).
15. Nagji and Tuff (2012).
16. Creating a Culture of Innovation (2014).
17. Jaruzelski and Dehoff (2010).
18. Werner and Souder (1997).
19. Jaruzelski and Dehoff (2010).
20. Booth, B. "Data Insight: Venture Capital returns and loss rates". *Forbes magazine Nov 7, 2012.* Also, "Venture Capital and Its 33% Success Rate" quoting data from Cambridge Associates.
21. Creating a Culture of Innovation (2014).
22. Coyne (n.d).
23. Leong (2013).

Chapter 7

1. "Another digital gold rush". The Economist May 12, 2011.
2. Massively Multiplayer Online Games.
3. All monetary figures have been shown in U.S. dollars instead of rupees to avoid dealing with large numbers.

4. CLV = \$550 × 0.78/0.02, where 0.78 is the gross margin (revenue net of 18 percent expenses), 550 is the ARRA, and 0.02 is the churn.

5. Negative churn occurs when increase of revenue due to new customers is greater than the decrease in revenue due to customers leaving.

Chapter 8

1. Armstrong and Baron (1998).

2. For product companies, effort (input) results in a software product. However, once the product is ready what is sold to the customer is only a license. In that respect, it is more akin to a service than a tangible product.

3. *Cf.* Gary (2001); Grote (2005).

4. Narrow curve means lower standard deviation, which means that the gap between top and bottom performers is smaller.

5. Repenning and Sterman (2001).

6. Big players like Accenture, HCL, Wipro, Microsoft, IBM and Infosys have all moved away from the bell curve. *Cf.* "Accenture too drops bell curve appraisals". The Economic Times. Jul 27, 2015. Also, "HCL begins shift from bell curve appraisals towards feedback-based system". The Economic Times. Oct 19, 2015.

7. Author and well-known business consultant Ram Charan tells companies that they have to adapt to the millennials: "I tell them you can't fire them. They will fire you. We have to give up most of the hierarchical structures and use digitisation for that. If you do not do that, you will get left behind. It's going to happen in the next three years. Millennials have skills that older people don't have." (IBM and Infosys reject bell curve, more companies to follow suit. "The Economic Times." Feb 12, 2016. http://economictimes. indiatimes.com/jobs/ibm-and-infosys-reject-bell-curve-more-companies-to-follow-suit/articleshow/50953764.cms)

8. "Infosys creates 'super ninjas' for deeper connect with clients". The Economic Times, Dec 31, 2014.

9. "Sops for Infosys staff to maintain 'zero distance' with clients". The Economic Times. Sep 22, 2016.

10. App Revenue Statistics (2015).

11. 50 percent of IT companies will lose part of their work: Digital automation may take bulk of deals (2016).

12. The future of work: Coding automation set to rob jobs (2016).

13. IBM and Infosys reject bell curve, more companies to follow suit (2016).

14. For example, at Infosys, attrition has dropped from 20 to 13 percent.

15. IBM and Infosys reject bell curve, more companies to follow suit (2016).

Appendix 2

1. For product companies, effort (input) results in a software product. However, once the product is ready what is sold to the customer is only a license. In that respect it is more akin to R&D effort.

Appendix 3

1. Even when the credit card is provided free of charge the user is a customer of the platform "in a meaningful way" as explained later in this section
2. According to statista.com the figure is 5.7 million as of June 2016.

References

Books and Academic Papers

Anthony, S. (2013). How to Really Measure a Company's Innovation Prowess. *Harvard Business Review March 21, 2013.*

Armstrong M. and Baron A. (1998). Performance Management: The new realities. *London: CIPD.*

Barber, F & Strack, R (2005). The Surprising Economics of a "People Business". *Harvard Business Review, June 2005.*

Brehmer, B. 1980. In one word: Not from experience. *Acta Psychol. 45,* 223–241

Bromwich, M. (1990). *The case for strategic management accounting: The role of accounting information for strategy in competitive markets.* Accounting, Organisations and Society. 15 (1–2), 27–46.

Bromwich, M. and Bhimani, A. (1991). Strategic investment appraisal. *Management Accounting (US), Vol.72, No. 9,* pp. 45–48.

Cooper, R & Kaplan, R. S. (1988). *Measure Costs Right: Make the Right Decisions.* Harvard Business Review, September 1988

Daniel K, Hirshleifer D, & Subrahmanyam A. (1998). Investor Psychology and Security Market Under- and Overreactions. *The Journal Of Finance Vol. LIII, No. 6,* 1839–1885

Einhorn, H. J., and Hogarth, R. M. 1978. Confidence in judgment: Persistence of the illusion of validity. *Psychol. Rev. 85,* 395–416

Engwall M, and Jerbrant A. (2003). The resource allocation syndrome: the prime challenge of multi-project management? *International Journal of Project Management 21.*

Gary, L. (2001). For Whom the Bell Curve Tolls. *Harvard Management Review. November 2001*

Gervais S and Odean T (2001). Learning to be overconfident, The Review of Financial Studies Spring 2001 Vol. 14, No. 1, 1–27

Gervais S, Heaton JB, Odean T. (2011). Overconfidence, compensation contracts, and capital budgeting. *The Journal of Finance, Vol. 66, No. 5,* 1735–1777

Goel, AM and Thakor, AV. (2008). Overconfidence, CEO selection and corporate governance, *Journal of Finance 63,* 2737–2784.

Grote, D. (2005). *Forced Ranking: Making Performance Management Work.* Harvard Business School Press Boston, MA.

Heemstra, FJ. (1992). Software cost estimation. *Information and Software Technology 34 (10),* 627–639.

Houlihan, J. B., 1987. *International Supply Chain Management*. International Journal of Physical Distribution and Materials Management, vol. 17, no. 2, 51–66.

Innes J (1998) Strategic Management Accounting in Innes J (ed.) *Handbook of Management Accounting*, Gee Ch. 2

Jaruzelski, Barry & Dehoff, Kevin, The Global Innovation 1000: How the Top Innovators Keep Winning. *Booz & Company's annual study. Strategy+Business, Winter 2010 / Issue 61*

Kaplan RS, (1986). Must CIM be justified by faith alone? *Harvard Business Review Vol. 64, No. 2,* 87–95

Lederer, A.L., Prasad, J. (1993). Information systems software cost estimating: a current assessment. *Journal of Information Technology 8 (1),* 22–33.

Lederer, AL, Prasad, J. (1995). Causes of inaccurate software development cost estimates. *Journal of Systems and Software 31 (2),* 125–134

Lord, B. R. (1996). *Strategic Management Accounting: The emperor's new clothes?* Management Accounting Research 7(3): 347–366.

Magazinius, A., Börjesson, S., Feldt, R. (2012). Investigating intentional distortions in software cost estimation - An exploratory Study. *The Journal of Systems and Software 85,* 1770–1781

Magazinovic A and Pernstål J. (2008). Any other cost estimation inhibitors? *Proceedings of the Second ACM-IEEE international symposium on Empirical software engineering and measurement,* 233–242

Moløkken-Østvold, K., Jørgensen, M., Tanilkan, S.S., Gallis, H., Lien, A.C., Hove, S.E., 2004. A Survey on Software Estimation in the Norwegian Industry. *Proceedings of 10th International Symposium on Software Metrics,* pp. 208–219.

Nagji, Bansi & Tuff, Geoff. (2012). Managing Your Innovation Portfolio. *Harvard Business Review, May 2012*

Orfalea, Paul, & Marsh, Ann. (2007). *Copy This! : Lessons from a Hyperactive Dyslexic who Turned a Bright Idea Into One of America's Best Companies.* Workman Publishing Company, Inc. New York, NY

Porter, M. E. (1980). *Competitive Strategy: Techniques for Analyzing Industries and Competitors.* Free Press, NY

Porter, M. E. (1985). *The Competitive Advantage: Creating and Sustaining Superior Performance.* NY: Free Press

Repenning, NP, and Sterman, JD. (2001). Nobody Ever Gets Credit for Fixing Problems that Never Happened: Creating and Sustaining Process Improvement. *California Management Review 43/4 (Summer 2001),* 64–88.

Riley D (1987). *Competitive Cost Based Investment Strategies for Industrial Companies.* Manufacturing Issues. Booz, Allen, Hamilton, New York

Sauer, C., Cuthbertson, C., 2003. The State of IT Project Management in the UK 2002-2003. Tempelton College, University of Oxford

Shank, John K. and Govindarajan, Vijay. (2008) *Strategic Cost Management: The New Tool for Competitive Advantage*, The Free Press, New York, NY

Simpson, James & Muthler David. (1987). *Quality Costs: Facilitating the Quality Initiative*. Journal of Cost Management, 1, 1 (Spring). pp. 25–34

Subramanian G.H. and Breslawski S (1995). An empirical analysis of software effort estimates alternations. *Journal of Systems Software 31*. 135–141

Szakonyi, R. (1994). Measuring R&D Effectiveness - II. *Research Technology Management May/Jun 1994*

Werner B.M. & Souder W. E. (1997). Measuring R&D Performance - State of the Art. Research Technology Management, Mar/Apr 1997.

Newspaper and Online articles/reports

50 per cent of IT companies will lose part of their work: Digital automation may take bulk of deals. *The Economic Times Nov 21, 2016.* http://economictimes.indiatimes.com/tech/ites/50-per-cent-of-it-companies-will-lose-part-of-their-work-digital-automation-may-take-bulk-of-deals/articleshow/55537835.cms

Accenture too drops bell curve appraisals. *The Economic Times. Jul 27, 2015.* http://economictimes.indiatimes.com/news/international/business/accenture-too-drops-bell-curve-appraisals/articleshow/48230902.cms.

Another digital gold rush. *The Economist May 12, 2011* www.economist.com/node/18680048?story_id=18680048

App Revenue Statistics 2015. http://www.businessofapps.com/app-revenue-statistics/

Apple watcher Neil Cybart blog http://www.aboveavalon.com/notes/2016/5/11/apple-rd-reveals-a-pivot-is-coming

Booth, B. Data Insight: Venture Capital returns and loss rates. *Forbes magazine Nov 7, 2012.* http://www.forbes.com/sites/brucebooth/2012/11/07/data-insight-venture-capital-returns-and-loss-rates/#22160ca64408.

BT 500: India's Most Valuable Companies (2013). *Business Today, 2013 Rankings.* http://businesstoday.intoday.in/story/business-today-top-500-companies-india-2013-rankings-intro/1/199729.html

Coyne, Tom. *Effectiveness, Efficiency, and Adaptability – The Three Keys to Performance Measurement.* http://www.tomcoyne.org/resources/ThreeKeyPerformanceMetrics.pdf

Craig Maxwell, Corporate VP (Technology and Innovation) Parker Hannifin Corp quoted in *The Future of R&D: Leveraging Innovation.* IndustryWeek, Apr 14, 2008. http://www.industryweek.com/companies-amp-executives/future-rd-leveraging-innovation

Creating a Culture of Innovation - A Google for Work perspective. *2014 Google Inc. Company document.* http://lp.google-mkto.com/rs/google/images/WP-

Creating-Culture-Innovation.pdf?mkt_tok=3RkMMJWWf
F9wsRolv67Jc%2B%2FhmjTEU5z16e0vWqC0gpx41El3
fuXBP2XqjvpVQcZnNLjORw8FHZNpywVWM
8TILtQYt8FtKAzgAG0%3D

For All its Repurchases, IBM Isn't a Factor in Buyback ETFs. *ETFtrends.
com, July 21, 2014.* Quoted in Yahoo Finance http://finance.yahoo.com/
news/repurchases-ibm-isn-t-factor-122043582.html. The aggressive share
repurchase strategy of IBM is probably the reason for the "financial
engineering" accusation quoted in the case study

Hall, Stephen et al. 2012. How to put your money where your strategy is.
McKinsey Article March 2012. http://www.mckinsey.com/businessfunctions
/strategyandcorporatefinance/ourinsights/howtoputyourmoneywhere
yourstrategyis

HCL begins shift from bell curve appraisals towards feedback-based system. *The
Economic Times. Oct 19, 2015.* http://economictimes.indiatimes.com/tech/
ites/hcl-begins-shift-from-bell-curve-appraisals-towards-feedback-based-
system/articleshow/49446096.cms, etc.

IBM and Infosys reject bell curve, more companies to follow suit. *The
Economic Times. Feb 12, 2016.* http://economictimes.indiatimes.com/
jobs/ibm-and-infosys-reject-bell-curve-more-companies-to-follow-suit/
articleshow/50953764.cms

Infosys creates 'super ninjas' for deeper connect with clients. *The Economic Times,
Dec 31, 2014.* http://economictimes.indiatimes.com/tech/ites/infosys-creates-
super-ninjas-for-deeper-connect-with-clients/articleshow/45697256.
cms?prtpage=1

Infosys Plunges After Murthy's Sales Growth Outlook. *BloombergBusiness, March
13, 2014.* http://www.bloomberg.com/news/articles/2014-03-13/infosys-
plunges-after-murthy-s-sales-growth-outlook

Leong, Kathy Chin. Google Reveals Its 9 Principles of Innovation. *Fast Company,
Nov. 20, 2013.* https://www.fastcompany.com/3021956/how-to-be-a-success-
at-everything/googles-nine-principles-of-innovation.

McKinsey Quarterly February 2007

Murthy concerned over decline in Infosys' growth. *Rediff.com/business. March
13, 2014.* http://www.rediff.com/business/slide-show/slide-show-1-tech-
murthy-concerned-over-decline-in-infosys-growth/20140313.htm

Ram Charan (As quoted in "IBM and Infosys reject bell curve, more companies
to follow suit". *The Economic Times. Feb 12, 2016.* http://economictimes.
indiatimes.com/jobs/ibm-and-infosys-reject-bell-curve-more-companies-to-
follow-suit/articleshow/50953764.cms)

Sops for Infosys staff to maintain 'zero distance' with clients. *The Economic Times. Sep 22, 2016.* http://economictimes.indiatimes.com/tech/ites/sops-for-infosys-staff-to-maintain-zero-distance-with-clients/articleshow/54454150.cms

Stop Hating IBM: It's Enormously Profitable. *Blue Harbinger. Oct. 29, 2015.* http://seekingalpha.com/article/3619316-stop-hating-ibm-its-enormously-profitable

The 2015 Five Key Performance Indicators for Greater Financial Success. *Service Performance Insight, LLC. Research Note. August 2015.*

The future of work: Coding automation set to rob jobs. *The Times of India, Feb 8, 2016.* http://timesofindia.indiatimes.com/city/chennai/The-future-of-work-Coding-automation-set-to-rob-jobs/articleshowprint/50894999.cms?null

Venture Capital and Its 33% Success Rate. Blogpost quoting data from Cambridge Associates. http://jtangovc.com/venture-capital-and-its-33-success-rate/vc-hit-rate/

Index

OTHER TITLES IN THE MANAGERIAL ACCOUNTING COLLECTION

Kenneth A. Merchant, University of Southern California, Editor

- *Revenue Management: A Path to Increased Profits, Second Edition* by Ronald J. Huefner
- *Cents of Mission: Using Cost Management and Control to Accomplish Your Goal* by Dale R. Geiger
- *Sustainability Reporting: Getting Started, Second Edition* by Gwendolen B. White
- *Lies, Damned Lies, and Cost Accounting: How Capacity Management Enables Improved Cost and Cash Flow Management* by Reginald Tomas Lee, Sr.
- *Strategic Management Accounting: Delivering Value in a Changing Business Environment Through Integrated Reporting* by Sean Stein Smith

Announcing the Business Expert Press Digital Library

Concise e-books business students need for classroom and research

This book can also be purchased in an e-book collection by your library as

- a one-time purchase,
- that is owned forever,
- allows for simultaneous readers,
- has no restrictions on printing, and
- can be downloaded as PDFs from within the library community.

Our digital library collections are a great solution to beat the rising cost of textbooks. E-books can be loaded into their course management systems or onto students' e-book readers.
The **Business Expert Press** digital libraries are very affordable, with no obligation to buy in future years. For more information, please visit **www.businessexpertpress.com/librarians**. To set up a trial in the United States, please email **sales@businessexpertpress.com**.

www.ingramcontent.com/pod-product-compliance
Lightning Source LLC
Chambersburg PA
CBHW050113210326
41519CB00015BA/3946